Horror Stories

Compilation of **Real** Police Encounters.

BY: DAVID M. CURTIS

© **Copyright 2017 -Night Terror Publishing All rights reserved.**

In no way is it legal to reproduce, duplicate, or transmit any part of this document in either electronic means or in printed format. Recording of this publication is strictly prohibited and any storage of this document is not allowed unless with written permission from the publisher. All rights reserved.

The information provided herein is stated to be truthful and consistent, in that any liability, in terms of inattention or otherwise, by any usage or abuse of any policies, processes, or directions contained within is the solitary and utter responsibility of the recipient reader. Under no circumstances will any legal responsibility or blame be held against the publisher for any reparation, damages, or monetary loss due to the information herein, either directly or indirectly.

Respective authors own all copyrights not held by the publisher.

Legal Notice:

This book is copyright protected. This is only for personal use. You cannot amend, distribute, sell, use, quote or paraphrase any part or the content within this book without the consent of the author or copyright owner. Legal action will be pursued if this is breached.

Disclaimer Notice:

Please note the information contained within this document is for educational and entertainment purposes only. Every attempt has been made to provide accurate, up to date and reliable complete information. No warranties of any kind are expressed or implied. Readers acknowledge that the author is not engaging in the rendering of legal, financial, medical or professional advice.

By reading this document, the reader agrees that under no circumstances are we responsible for any losses, direct or indirect, which are incurred as a result of the use of information contained within this document, including, but not limited to, —errors, omissions, or inaccuracies.

Table of Contents

INTRODUCTION **6**

CHAPTER 1 .... **10**
    Exorcism in Indianapolis 10

CHAPTER 2 .... **20**
    The Watcher.. 20

CHAPTER 3 .... **28**
    The Death of Elisa 28

CHAPTER 4 .... **37**
    Utah Murder.. 37

CHAPTER 5 .... **45**
    The Phone Stalker.. 45

CHAPTER 6 .... **52**
    The Voodoo Torturers 52

CHAPTER 7 .... **60**
    The Man Who Hated God 60

CHAPTER 8 .... **67**
    Nasty Neighbour Blues 67

CHAPTER 9 .... **76**
    Everyone Meet Bob 76

CHAPTER 10 .... **82**

    The Housing Development Site 82

Chapter 11 .... **89**

    The Abandoned Hospital 89

Chapter 12 .... **97**

    The Keyholder 97

Chapter 13 .... **102**

    The Church That Was Haunted 102

Chapter 14 .... **108**

    The Children in The Attic 108

Chapter 15 .... **113**

    Revelations of a Victim 113

Chapter 16 .... **118**

    The Little Girl 118

Chapter 17 .... **122**

    Shadows and Cameras 122

Chapter 18 .... **128**

    The Red Ribbon 128

Chapter 19 .... **134**

    Dark Shadows 134

Chapter 20 .... **140**

    Vanishing Calls 140

Chapter 21 .... **148**

CRIME SCENE PHOTOS	148
CHAPTER 21	**154**
THE SWAMP	154
CHAPTER 23	**162**
PLAY BALL	162
CHAPTER 24	**168**
THE LOCKED DOOR	168
CHAPTER 25	**174**
THE FIRE OF THE LIGHTHOUSE	174
CONCLUSION	**181**
CAN YOU HELP ME OUT?	**186**
CHECK OUT MY OTHER BOOKS	**188**

Introduction

Nowadays, horror stories are more and more popular. From Alfred Hitchcock to Stephen King, lots of mystery and tales of horror have entered our lives in multiple ways and formats. A great number of top-rating TV series', movies and books have been specially made to thrill people at home. However, all of these types of entertainment media have one thing in common – when you close the book, turn off the TV and everything is over, you come back to reality knowing that what you just read or viewed is fiction. But just to let you in on a big secret, all of the stories included in this book are true accounts; they happened to real people, just like you and me. There is no certainty that all these events are truly over, or how they really happened. Mystery is part of our daily lives, just like in these stories.

Moreover, the role of the lawful authorities in these stories is fundamental, as they are the ones who are responsible for finding out the truth. Continue reading to find out about the most strange and ghastly events that police officers had to investigate, all in the line of duty. Among these stories you can find mysteries, unknown watchers and callers, demonic possessions, and much more. Sometimes, after some research, the guilty parties and the answers are eventually found. However, that is not always the case. This book delves into strange enigma in seemingly textbook investigations that the police find themselves in, sometimes without knowing how to proceed, and frequently, not knowing with certainty what really happened.

Also featured in this book, you will find stories from all over the world. From strange happenings in a hotel in Los Angeles to a strange murder in Utah. Not to mention weird neighbors in New Jersey and multiple exorcisms in Indianapolis. Unbelievable psychotics in London, England, like Voodoo torturers and the man who hates God. All these cases were true and featured in the news, as they made headlines when they first happened. They shook everyone who read about the stories to the core, as they were unimaginable and truly horrific. There are no safe places, as terror can take over any refuge and any home. There are no safe hours because the unimaginable can also happen in the bright light of day, not just in the dead of night.

For narrative and fictional purposes, the names of the persons in the cases have been altered, to preserve the identities of the people involved. Nevertheless, the dates and locations are not. These reports are fictionalized in order for you to find them more enjoyable and exciting, but all these events took place in real life and were investigated and appeared in the newspapers and/or, were telecast.

Are you ready? Because coming up next, you will find the most terrifying stories that just happened in the recent years. These stories are real, based on true events and written under the guidelines of real investigations made by the police. Therefore, everything that you will read here actually happened to a real person, just like you and me, not a very long time ago. Come and sit a while with me and read about these horrifying stories, if you dare...

Chapter 1

Exorcism in Indianapolis

"I have never seen something like that, truly. At first, I thought it was a sort of prank, or exaggeration in order to get some money. I really thought they were making us waste our time, I have been through that, it happens to me a lot in my daily work. But now I can tell you that this was all for real. Before this, I didn't believe in the supernatural, but now I can truly tell you that I believe that demonic spirits exist." – These are the words of the actual police captain of the Gary Police Department. As he explained this, he felt the necessity to narrate the case from the very start.

In late 2011, a family moved into a small, one-story home on a quiet neighborhood in Gary, Indiana. Just a normal family, comprised of a mother with her three children and the grandmother, all looking to find a place to peacefully settle into. However, this optimistic outlook did not last long. Just a month later, Mrs. A started noticing some strange things happening in their home on Carolina Street in Gary. On a cold December day, a swarm of flies mysteriously invaded their screened-in porch. Despite their efforts to get rid of them, the flies continuously appeared and kept coming back. Although she thought it strange, she did not feel alarmed. However, things quickly started to get creepy. Every night, the family heard footsteps on the basement stairs and the slamming of the kitchen door, but when they turned the lights on and looked around, no one was there. Moreover, Mrs. A started to hear barking at night as well, and when she would get up to see where the dog was that was making all that noise, she could not spot any dog anywhere near the house. One night, in her living room, Mrs. A noticed a shadowy figure. Upon inspection, nothing and no one was there, except for some mysterious wet boot footprints.

Needless to say, uncertainty turned to fear. A couple of months later, while the family was mourning a loved one with a group of friends, Mrs. A found her twelve-year-old child unconscious and levitating over the bed. Frantic, she called for her mother to help her. At that moment in their house, no one could believe what was happening; everyone who was present prayed because they had never seen anything like that. Later, the child finally descended back onto the bed and woke up. She could not remember a single thing. All the people who were in the house that night refused to come back ever again.

Mrs. A's mother told her daughter then, "We have to do something about this. It was not common, what happened. I mean, it is not every day that you find a child floating over a bed. I did not know what that was, but we certainly could not fix it by ourselves, we needed help. But no one would help us. I remember going to several churches, but no one listened to us."

After frantic and non-stop appeals for help, Mrs. A and her mother were finally advised by an official from one of the churches that they sought help from. The church official said the house had evil spirits in it and that they should not waste another second, they needed to clean their home with bleach and ammonia, then use oil to draw crosses all around the house, on the doors and windows. Following the advice of the church official, Mrs. A put olive oil on the hands and feet of her three children, and then drew crosses with the oil on their foreheads.

Yet, after all that, they still experienced unsettling and strange situations, forcing them to look for even more kind souls who would help them. Mrs. A and her mother were able to talk to some clairvoyants who told the two women that the house was full of demons, and that the best solution was to move. However, since moving was not an option for the family, Mrs. A decided to follow another psychic's advice to make an altar in the basement.

After that, Mrs. A thought that everything would go back to normal, but she was wrong, so very wrong. Just three days after the altar was made, the demonic possessions began. Not only did they start to happen more systematically, but they also became more and more violent. Mrs. A reported to the police that she and her three children were being possessed by demons on a regular basis and it was driving them all insane. In 2012, things got even worse. One of the children threatened to kill his brother. Everything was out of control and neither the children nor Mrs. A knew what to do. They were terrified because the supernatural events continued to happen even while impartial, outside investigators were right there in the house with them, watching and observing. These supernatural events were happening in front of the authorities but everyone was helpless with what to do.

Soon after that, the children were taken to a hospital and separated from their mother. While in the hospital, their personalities became more and more strange day by day. The nurses said that the seven-year-old youngest boy would sit alone talking to an imaginary friend and describe how it felt to be killed. Other professionals in the hospital said that the twelve-year-old eldest girl told them that she sometimes felt as though she were being choked and held down so she could not move, or speak. Moreover, she also said that she heard voices telling her that she would not see her family again and that she would not live more than twenty minutes. Their grandmother recounted that one of the children was seen flying out of the bathroom as if he had been thrown by someone. On another instance, the eldest girl hit a headboard as if it was thrown at her, causing a head wound and needed to be taken to the emergency room for her to get stitches.

Child Services interviewed the family and found some very disturbing statements coming from the children. The case manager initially said that Mrs. A and the children were mentally stable and healthy. No bruises or other marks were observed. Later on, however, while the family was being interviewed at the hospital, the seven-year-old started growling and baring his teeth while his eyes rolled back into his head. The boy then locked his hands around his brother's throat in a fatal choking movement and would not let go until the adults in the room pried his hands open. Later that day, both of the boys were taken to a room in order for the authorities to ask them a few questions. The seven-year-old started growling again and told his brother that it was time to die. His voice also suddenly changed and he told his brother, in a deep and unnatural voice, "I will kill you."

There were other horrific manifestations that the children displayed at the hospital. Among them was when a nurse claimed that she saw the nine-year-old casting a weird grin, before suddenly walking backwards, straight up the ceiling, before flipping over his grandmother, all while never letting go of her hand. The nurse ran, petrified, out of the hospital room. After the children's confinement and testing at the hospital, Mrs. A and the family went to one of their relative's houses near their own home. However, Mrs. A lost custody of her kids when child services told her that the children were being neglected, as they had not been going to school. It was at this time that the Reverend Maginot was called upon by the hospital to help out the misfortune-stricken family.

Maginot, accompanied by other priests and some police officers, first started performing small exorcisms on Mrs. A. His main goal was to repel the spirits and make them go away. When this did not seem to work, he blessed the home and performed bigger, more intense exorcism sessions whereupon he learned the identities of the evil spirits that were haunting the home.

Finally, in June of 2012, the good Reverend Maginot conducted a ceremony in Latin at the controversial house of Mrs. A. That time, the police were not present as witnesses, but some of his fellow priests were there to help and assist him. He said Mrs. A. convulsed while he condemned the demons but did not move at all throughout the prayer. In the midst of the exorcism, Mrs. A fell into a deep sleep, at which point the Reverend said a thanksgiving.

Mrs. A did not see Maginot again after the exorcisms. She returned to her home in Indianapolis with her mother. The police also said that records show no paranormal disturbances prior and after Mrs. A's family took residence in the house. Moreover, the current tenant of the house said that he had never heard anything like that before but felt less skeptical when he heard that the church was involved. The house on Carolina Street and the terrible stories about what happened within evolved into becoming a local legend, and even became a tourist-attraction of sorts.

Later that year, Mrs. A. regained custody of her children. "The day I reunited with my children was the happiest day of my life. We were finally together, after such a long time and after such terrible things," she said with a smile on her face. Everybody happily rejoiced and was overcome with joy during this positive time. After that, Mrs. A and her family felt safe in their new home and her family lived a much-deserved happy and haunting-free life.

Chapter 2

The Watcher

-So, what happened miss? Tell me. Feel free to say anything, the more you talk, the more you can help us help you. Any detail you remember is very valuable.

-Ok, this started some weeks ago when my family and I moved to our new house, out here in Westfield. Since then, we have been receiving some really disturbing messages nonstop. We do not know what to do; we tried to avoid them, but there are just too many, and they are too disturbing. I cannot even describe them, truly terrible...

In 2015, a typical family moved to New Jersey in order to pursue their dreams. They had seen and bought the perfect house in the beautiful and picturesque town of Westfield. They had invested over 1 million dollars in this house, and that represented everything they longed for and wanted. A large, six room house in Union County with a front and back yard, a porch and plants everywhere. This meant more space for the kids to grow in, a garden for the kids to play in, and a quiet and perfect neighborhood for the kids to go to school. Everything seemed perfect for this average American family. So far everything was going well and according to plan for this family. They had everything they could ever want, or so it seemed. However, once they moved into this dreamy and perfectly-crafted new home, everything changed, and not in the way they had imagined it would.

-Slow down Miss; I cannot understand you if you talk that fast. Calm down and breathe. Tell me everything that happened, from the beginning. Talk slower, please. I cannot understand you; please slow down, Miss.

-Well, it all started the very first day we moved in. We arrived on a sunny day and everything seemed perfect, the house and the neighborhood looked more beautiful than from what I remembered. As we settled into the house and walked around our new place, we noticed a letter on the living room floor. We thought that the real state agency had left it there for us, or maybe that someone just forgot it there. However, it wasn't from the agency. That's when it started. Atrocious letters continued to come almost every day. My husband thought that they were coming from some kids pulling a prank.

-Continue Miss, what did the letters say?

-It's terrible; I can't...

These petrifying letters arrived as surely as the newspaper did for the family. They came every day and each day they got worse. They came from someone who called himself The Watcher. He stated in his letters that he was called that because that was what he did, what he was meant to do – to watch over the place and to care for the house. They didn't know the man and they did not see him. They had no clue as to who would drop these letters into their home. Untiring, The Watcher did not miss a day. His apparent purpose was to get that family out of there, at all cost.

The Watcher stated in his letters that he was the one who should be living in the house, as the house had been in his family for decades. Claiming the property as his own, he said in one of the letters that he was put in charge of watching and waiting for the second coming. He had a family legacy to follow that could not be avoided. **Fixated on** this idea, this mysterious man kept sending more and more letters. These letters were true cause for alarm as they contained death threats directed at the family which escalated with each terrifying note.

-And tell me, Miss, did the letters ever stop or did you ever notice someone strange who could have been this watcher man you are telling me about?

-No... I cannot understand how, how someone could be so mean. We did not do anything to him; we just bought a house. We moved there like anyone that moves into any new house; we have the papers that say the house is ours.

-I see. But you did not answer me, have you seen anyone suspicious?

-No, nothing.

The Watcher's letters were even more threatening and terrifying as he continued spying on them. He knew personal details about the family, who they were, where they came from, and what they did. In his letters, he would say horrifying things like: "Have they found out what's in the walls yet?" and "I am pleased to know your names now, and the name of the young blood you have brought me." Obviously, The Watcher was a menacing presence.

The family didn't know what to do or how to react because clearly, it wasn't a child's prank anymore. They were scared of going inside their house and finding a new letter, or even worse, encountering The Watcher. With things getting terribly out of hand and not really knowing the extent of what this intruder was capable of, the family went to the police.

The police conducted an exhaustive investigation of the circumstances and evidence provided, but they could not find out the identity of this strange perpetrator. Months of investigation did nothing to shed light or provide any leads to solving this case. It would seem that The Watcher did not even exist, at least not in our normal world. The police said that the letters were classified as a "disorderly person's crime". Even the neighbors couldn't believe what was happening, claiming that they would be very angry if the previous owners had not mentioned any knowledge of such a disturbing factor to the current family that had bought the place.

In the end, the family was forced to move. There was no other choice. They knew that someone seemingly invisible was watching them, stalking them, threatening them and that the family's lives were at stake. There was nothing the police could do to protect them.

The couple who owned the New Jersey house on Westfield were finally able to rent their controversial home , after more than two years of it being vacant, in February 2017 and the current renter who goes by the name "Chris" is the owner of three dogs and is allegedly not bothered by any "stalker" threats or Watcher actions.

Will the new tenant of the house be subject to the stalker terror that "The Watcher" will bring? Only time will tell.

Chapter 3

The Death of Elisa

"After January 31, she never called again. Everything was going fine, at least that was what she said. Elisa said everything was going fine; she called every day. She sent pictures and everything, and it suddenly stopped. We are really scared, we do not know what to do, and we just want to know if our daughter is ok." – This was what Elisa's mother lamented over the phone, as the police tried to calm her down. The authorities immediately started looking for her without realizing what troubling mystery they would stumble upon.

Elisa was not unlike every other young woman; she longed to travel and explore the world as much as she could. She was an average girl, with average height and looks. Brown hair, wide smile and a look of youth and hope in her eyes. She had always behaved in a normal way and and showed no signs of mental psychosis. In January 2013, Elisa decided to go on a trip and, not knowing how things would turn out for her, she decided to go sightseeing in the West Coast and enjoy the warmer weather over there. But once she got to Los Angeles, everything changed for the worse.

Elisa had been taking pictures, happily documenting her adventure by making personal videos and calling her parents every single day. However, at the end of the month, these updates by Elisa suddenly stopped. The police started to look all over for her, her parents even flew out to California in order to help in the search for Elisa. But after numerous days of looking, not a trace of her was found with not even the slightest clue as to where Elisa could have gone. She seemed to have simply vanished. She was last seen in the lobby of the Cecil Hotel in downtown Los Angeles, and after that, no one ever saw her alive again.

The local police put in a lot of manpower and used all their investigative skills to look for Elisa, but no trace was ever found. They had absolutely nothing, no clue of where she might be. However, the cops noticed something in the elevator CCTV footage of the Cecil Hotel which they definitely found kind of strange. The video showed Elisa just a few hours before her approximated disappearance. But rather than give some answers, the video presented some images that were truly disturbing and raised more questions rather than providing much-needed answers.

In the footage, the police saw that Elisa entered the elevator and pressed the button for more than four floors. With anxious movements, as the lift opened at each floor, she peeked out of the elevator and quickly entered back in. This odd behavior happened repeatedly. Frantically, she touched the buttons over and over again as she went in and out, making curious hand gestures.

By her body language, Elisa seemed to be engaged in conversation with someone or something that cannot be seen on the CCTV camera footage. After several times, the elevator doors opened and closed, and for the last time, she went out of the elevator and off-frame from the CCTV footage view, but never returned.

The police came up with some theories after viewing the video. In the footage, the police reported that she was clearly seen making strange movements and appearing to talk to invisible people. Moreover, she also moved in a very suspicious way, peering around the corner outside of the elevator, staying in the innermost corner when she was inside and constantly opening and closing the doors. Some thought that she may have been suffering from a psychotic episode. The possibility of an unknown assailant outside of the camera's angle was also considered. Others went even further and even talked about a possible demonic possession.

This disturbing CCTV footage was the only trace of Elisa since she disappeared into thin air. Providing little answers, the video only served to make things more complex.

A few days later, the police received some complaints from the same hotel. These complaints were about the water supply of the hotel and some rooms. A woman, staying in the Cecil hotel for more than a week, during the period that coincided with the investigation on Elisa's disappearance, complained to hotel staff that the shower was disgusting and terrible. Apparently, the water that came out was color black at first but after a few seconds, it returned to a clear color. This lady also said that the water tasted horrible and was impossible to drink. She insisted that the water had a peculiar taste about it and that she could not find the words to describe it. At first, she thought that it was just the way the water was in Los Angeles, but when it became too much for her to take, she finally had to complain about it. Soon after, more guests gave similar complaints about the color and taste of the water flowing in their hotel room bathroom taps.

On February 19, after numerous complaints, one of the hotel employees decided to take a look and inspect the water tank. Using a ladder, he climbed to the roof to investigate what might be spoiling the water supply of The Cecil Hotel. The water tank of the hotel was enormous and had a heavy metal opening. Upon his inspection, he revealed the shocking sight of poor Elisa's body. Bloated in death, floating inside the water tank, was the unmistakable girl from the elevator. She was dead, naked, and decomposing in the tank. Her possessions and clothes were found inside the tank with her, and the autopsy showed that her death appeared to be purely an accidental drowning.

However later on, the police uncovered some very strange circumstances about the hotel's past. Apparently, Elisa's case was just one of a handful of shocking incidents that took place at the Cecil Hotel.

The strange history of the single room where Elisa was billeted goes back to 1962, when a woman who had stayed in the hotel took her own life when she jumped out of her bedroom window. But she didn't just kill herself; she also accidentally killed a person who was passing by below her window on the street, as she fatally fell on him, causing both their deaths.

In 1985, a guest named Richard Ramirez lived on one of the floors of the hotel for several months. It came to pass that he was the serial killer famously known as the "Night Stalker". During those years, Ramirez allegedly stalked and killed fourteen women. His murders were characterized by the amount of slashes and cuts on the victims.

The horrific history of the Cecil Hotel went from bad to worst in 1991, when an international killer named Jack Unterweger also lived there for some months. It was during his stay at the hotel that he was suspected of murdering three prostitutes in that area of Los Angeles. In 1994, police investigations sent him to jail where he soon committed suicide.

Considering the sinister history of the Cecil Hotel, the case of Elisa suddenly takes on a very different and sinister tone. All evidence collected during the police investigations did not shed any light on why she was behaving that way in the elevator CCTV footage, how she got into the water tank, and, ultimately, why she died. While this case will always remain a mystery for The Cecil Hotel (now presently known as "Stay On Main"), considering its violent history, one thing that seems plausible is that this hotel is truly cursed and will forever haunt and maybe even kill its visitors. Potential Hotel Guests, you have been warned!

Chapter 4

Utah Murder

In Springfield, Utah, a nineteen-year-old teen returned in the evening to his family home as he always did, every night. He came with his girlfriend, and when he arrived home, expecting to find both his parents and his three siblings, he found nothing. The lights were off and there was total silence. No one was there; there were no noises or movements, nothing. After checking the rest of the house, he went to look in the main bedroom, his parent's room. It was locked from the inside.

Immediately, he called his grandmother for help and she came as soon as she could. She forced her way inside the bedroom and neither she nor her grandson could believe what they saw. They found five dead bodies in the room, his parents Benjamin and Kristi Strack and his three younger siblings were all unmoving and lifeless.

Although there was no note, it appeared like a suicide. The oldest son did find a to-do list that made it seem as if they were about to go on a vacation. Among the items on the list included: look for someone to watch the house, feed the pets, and buy some sunscreen. Because of this, the police found the homicide incredibly strange. Why would two reasonable and loving parents who were planning a vacation for their family, suddenly and for no apparent reason, kill themselves?

When the police got to the scene in the small town near Salt Lake City, they found containers of empty medications near the bodies. These jars had contained cold and flu medication, allergy medication, sleeping medication, painkillers and cherry flavored methadone. But that was not everything they found; they also spotted a plastic container filled with some yellow substance, which, upon inspection, was a lethal mixture of drugs. The police were understandably taken aback with all the evidence on the scene and they would later deem this 911 call where the authorities responded, as one of the most tragic murder-suicide cases in Utah's history.

The age of the three dead children ranged from 11 – 14 years old. Being minors, it could not be ascertained whether they voluntarily agreed to the suicide. The police said it was unclear how they could have consumed the drug cocktail. Therefore, the deaths of the two younger kids were labeled as homicides while the third and oldest one remained uncertain. But without a doubt, the police catalogued the deaths of both parents as suicides.

The autopsy said that the mother had a great amount of diphenhydramine, an antihistamine, and methadone, plus dextrorphan and doxylamine. Her husband had a toxic level of heroin in his system, whereas the children had consumed the same drugs as their mother. The police, together with close acquaintances, believed that the previous mental health of the couple needed further investigation to find out why they had premeditated this fatal family situation. .

For a very long time, the police gathered no information. Everyone was still clueless as to what could have driven the Strack couple to make such a tragic decision. After a few more months of investigations and inquiries with family members, a few horrifying details came up. Apparently, a convicted killer may have convinced the parents that an apparent apocalypse was coming.

The police reported that the people that surrounded the family heard them say they were worried about all the evils that were in the world and that they longed to escape a pending and possible apocalypse. Further investigations revealed that the mother, Kristi Strack, had written letters to one of the most infamous convicted killers in the state, Dan Lafferty. This man was found guilty in 1984 for violently killing his sister-in-law and her one-year-old. At that time, Lafferty said he had killed them because his brother, Ron Lafferty, claimed that he had received a message from God that said that he should do so. The discovery of the letters written by the mother to the killer convict further revealed that both parents had become very close friends with this convicted criminal and that they had talked to him during several prison visits. These encounters, however, ceased in 2008.

Police also found a letter written by one of the dead children, the fourteen-year-old, bequeathing all his personal belongings to a friend. The police said that this was a farewell letter but that it did not contain any information about the reasons or the method of the murder. In the letter, the child said to his friend that he would no longer exist on this earth.

The way the bodies of the children were found suggested that they were first put to sleep before they expired. The police also deduced that the nineteen-year-old eldest son was not included in the murder-suicide plan because he was grown up already and engaged to be married in just a few months.

During further investigation, the police found some more troubling information about the Strack couple. Apparently, the mother, Kristi, had problems with heroin some years before. At the time of the suicide, she was receiving methadone treatments to help lessen the addiction. Also, the father, Benjamin Strack, skipped worked regularly. A man that worked with him told the police that for some years he did not go to work for long periods of time, claiming he was helping his wife. Just before the suicide, he had been absent for more than a week.

It was at this point that the police investigations ran into a wall. No other new evidence presented itself to help completely solve the case and answer the questions on why the Strack couple did what they did to themselves and their three young children.

The question as to why these parents did what they did may never be answered. Moreover, whether or not they convinced the children to do the same and kill themselves, will also remain an unanswered question.

This tragedy in Utah will forever be shadowed in darkness and mystery, with the truth never able to see the light of day.

Chapter 5

The Phone Stalker

In 2007, the Washington Police received multiple reports from several families that had one big and terrifying similarity. All these families received phone calls containing death threats. The person or persons who made the phone calls knew everything about their victims, from what they were doing, what they were wearing, their names, their location at the time of the call and much more.

These three families also said that these calls came in the middle of the night, with threats of killing their children, their pets and their grandparents. Not only that, but the caller also knew when the kids were at school and when family members were alone in their homes. And, more terrifying, the families received voice mails from this unknown caller where they could hear recordings of their own private conversations, including some with the police and private detectives. The ominous voice over the phone seemed to know everything, and every detail was used against them.

After months of constant investigation and research, the police had nothing, no clue as to who could be the voice behind these terrible and terrifying calls. They did not have information on who could be making them and, consequently, they seemed powerless to stop it.

One family in particular, the K's, had been receiving these calls for months. It all started in February that year when their sixteen-year-old daughter's cellphone started texting and sending messages by itself. At first, they thought the phone had gone crazy, sending messages by itself, but they were wrong. Then, they thought the daughter might be exaggerating the details, as phones logically cannot do things by themselves. Shortly after that, the threatening calls escalated wherein a scratchy and deep voice would come on the receiver saying the whole family's throats would be slit. Everything then changed dramatically for the family.

This was the beginning of the K's nightmares. The calls never ceased and they only got worse. As the police started investigating this case, as well as the calls made to the other families, they noticed that when they traced the phone calls, they all came back to the K's own phones. It appeared as if the threatening calls made originated from the very phones of the K's family. The police reported that this unknown caller was using their own phones to spy on them. The mother, at first, surmised that the calls seemed liked some kid making a prank. But after a while, the threats became really graphic and disturbing. One of the many messages that they received said: "I know where you are. I know where you live. I am going to kill you". The family said that these calls were constant and that if a day passed without a single threat, then it was a good day indeed.

The family claimed that their cell phones would switch on by themselves and that they changed their ringtones automatically too. It would seem that the phones were possessed. Sometime after these calls began, the K's decided to install a new security system in their home due to the constant fear they felt. However, once the mother finished setting everything up, she received a voicemail in which the unknown caller stated that he knew the new security code.

As days passed, things kept getting worse. One time, the mother was slicing limes in the kitchen, and she received a call from this raspy voice saying he preferred lemons to limes. She was in shock. She looked everywhere, and found no one outside that could have been spying at her. Moreover, when the K's talked to the police, the threatening voice started giving warnings for the family that he knew they were talking to the cops and demanded they to stop talking to them. This ghastly voice seemed to be everywhere at every moment.

The K's didn't know what else to do; the calls never stopped, and the police did not know what else to do. They changed their accounts and switched their phones more than two times, but the calls were relentless. No matter what they did, they could not get the calls to stop. They became a daily torture that they could not escape.

The police were confounded. They had never seen such a case before. They contacted numerous police departments from other states, and they even reached out to the department of Homeland Security, **but they** still had no idea how to solve this case. Some experts told the cops that it was not that difficult to get into phones nowadays, but still, they had no idea how to trace that kind of hacking movement. No one had answers about what could be done. This activity, according to the police, was breaking a large number of laws, **not only because** of the death threats, but also because of the invasion of the family's private property.

Due to the amount of information that the caller possessed, the police suspected that the person responsible could be a member of their own family. At one time, the sixteen-year-old became a possible suspect. However, her parents stated that their daughter was not disturbed and that she could not have been responsible for all those calls since she was sometimes present during the moment when the calls took place. Nevertheless, the police were sure that it was a case that involved cyber-bullying and that it might be traced back to some wiz-kid's idea of a sick prank.

The situation did not seem to have a resolution, and the families continued to be terrorized by some unknown high-tech stalker in the supposed sanctuary and supposed safety of their own homes.

Chapter 6

The Voodoo Torturers

Christmas day 2010, London, England. An urgent call was made to the Paramedics because a woman found her young fifteen-year-old brother drowned in the bathroom tub. As she called for help, her husband desperately tried again and again to resuscitate the boy, but he had already died.

When the police got to the flat in Forest Gate, East London, they found the boy in the bathroom tub covered with several marks on his skin. But they were not simple scratches; he had deep cuts and bruises all over the body. It looked as if the boy had been tortured for days.

"It was an accident, I swear. It got out of our hands," said Mr. B, the husband of the victim's sister. He looked in fear at his wife, Mrs. B, and at the police officer. As the policemen watched the couple with eyes of suspicion, they could not begin to imagine all the terrifying and horrible things that they were going to find out about this case in the next few days.

It all started a couple of days earlier with the beginning of the Christmas holiday. Like every year, Mrs. B and her four siblings would get together in their mother's house to celebrate this special time of year. They got together and ate, sang, and had a good time as a family. But on the Christmas of 2010, this was not the case. Quite the contrary, it was a week of unbelievably horrifying and disturbing family unrest gone wild.

Mr. and Mrs. B were both born in the Democratic Republic of Congo. She was a shop girl, and he was a football coach. They were an average couple who were deeply in love and happy with each other. Interestingly, they both believed in Kindoki and sorcery.

According to Wikipedia, Kindoki is thought by its believers to be a kind of witchcraft or possession by evil spirits where children are subjected to exorcisms that include beatings, starvation and submersion in water.

When Mr. and Mrs. B arrived at the flat in Forest Gate, they noticed something that called their attention. One of Mrs. B's brothers who was fifteen years old at the time, wet himself. It was a simple child's accident that meant nothing. However, Mr. and Mrs. B could not believe their eyes and became convinced that the boy was a witch and was possessed by evil spirits.

As the supposed older and wiser member of the family, Mr. B was determined to help Mrs. B's brother. In order to do that, he needed help from the rest of the family. He instructed the other kids to fast, pray and chant through several nights around Mrs. B's brother, in order to repel the evil spirits in his body.

However, things got out of hand when Mr. B started to act not only strangely but violently too. He was not just saying weird things and singing in a strange language, but he now started to take physical actions during the ritual. One night he told the rest of the siblings that he would throw them out the window in order to see how the witches fly. One of the siblings told the police that as he told them that, his eyes were filled with fury and that he looked violently at them as if possessed by some terrifying evil.

Both Mr. and Mrs. B believed that it was their job to rid the house of the evil spirits. As the husband and wife believed that it was incumbent upon them to cleanse and exorcise the house, the threats to the young siblings took a turn from bizarre to violent beyond any limit they had ever imagined.

According to the couple, Mrs. B's young teenaged brother, the one who they believed was a witch, was the sibling that needed to undergo through the rite of exorcism as he was the concentration of the evil in the house. They took him and beat him with a metal curtain rod and a weightlifting bar. They smashed ceramic tiles and glass bottles over his head, making a bloody, sticky opening that only got larger, cut after cut. They also used a hammer to knock out his teeth. In this way, the reign of terror of Mr. and Mrs. B had started. They used pliers to twist and tear parts of his ear, and they used chisels and knives to stab him constantly and slice his flesh. They even abused him with a mop. Rather than helping Mrs. B's brother be free of whatever evil spirit they believed was within him, the insane couple made him suffer and live out hell-on-earth in his young and short-lived existence.

The physical state in which the police found the boy was horrific. They found a screw in his bowel that they had forced him to swallow, and his fingers, hands and thighs had been smashed continuously with a claw hammer, leaving the bones broken and all his skin bruised. Apart from all that, the fifteen-year-old was missing a great number of teeth. Cuts covered his body, his face, his arms, his back and his legs. The boy was severely mutilated.

The police also found the boy's skull very damaged. His head was covered with cuts, and his throat was also badly hurt. The cops believed that his throat was injured because Mr. B shoved a weightlifting bar down it. And, as the police continued to look at the teenager's body, they found more and more terrifying wounds that gave an account of the systematic violence he had suffered at the hands of those he had once believed to be his loving family.

To make matters worse, both Mr. and Mrs. B attacked the other two sisters, and forced them to join in the violence against the boy. If the girls did not help them, they would punish them. If the couple believed they were not trying hard enough or that they were not doing the boy much pain, they would punish them much worse.

Mr. and Mrs. B forced all the siblings to hurt the boy and make him suffer; no one could escape their violence. Realizing one of the girls was only pretending to hit her brother because she did not want to hurt him, Mr. B forced a lightbulb down her throat as punishment. He also held her around the throat and held a knife to her chest, threatening and hurting her repeatedly.

During the course of this unimaginable torture period, the couple inflicted a total of one hundred and thirty wounds on Mrs. B's young brother, both external and internal. They made him suffer and go through inexplicable and inhuman suffering. The pain became too much for him to bear and he begged the couple over and over for them to kill him. As a result, the couple took him and left him in the bathroom tub to die.

"It was an accident, I swear. We did not mean for it to end this way," Mr. B continued saying to the police.

In trial, Mr. and Mrs. B were charged with murder and two counts of assault. Mrs. B denied all the charges against her while Mr. B admitted to the assault charges and manslaughter on the grounds of diminished capacity. Finally, they were both condemned to a minimum of thirty years in jail.

With this story we can wonder if there is truly a hell that can exist on Earth. Hell can happen even in the most normal places, sometimes even in the most mundane small family bathroom in the suburbs.

Chapter 7

The Man Who Hated God

In 2011, over a period of six weeks, two murders were committed. At first, the only similarity that both crimes had was the fact that both victims belonged to the clergy. The first one happened in January when frail Betty Y. was killed at her home in Bewdley, Worcs. The other crime was when Rev. John S. was murdered in his vicarage in Thornbury, South Glos.

At first, it seemed strange how two religious people could be murdered on dates so close to each other. With further investigation, this is what the police found out about both cases and their connection.

Mr. F was a lonesome man of about forty-nine years of age. He was an average male, with short brown hair and light-colored eyes. However, he had one abnormal fixation in life, which was to get revenge on the church and it's clergymen. Allegedly, Mr. F was a God-hating man and claimed he was against the institution of the church. He explained later on that his intense hate for the religious institution stemmed from the abuse delivered to him by a priest when he was but a child.

The police said that apparently, this conduct of Mr. F towards the church had been like that for some time. Investigations revealed that prior to the aforementioned murders, Mr. F had a series of other crimes and misdemeanors. Just a few weeks before, he had taken a trip to Canterbury where he attempted to kill the archbishop Rowan W., but was put off by security. In another incident the previous Christmas, Mr. F broke into a cottage near the vicarage while it was unattended and, with a knife, pinned a note on the table that said: "Be thankful you did not come back, or we would have killed you, Christian scum. I f***ing hate God."

With his rage increasing just a few days before the first murder, Mr. F allegedly sent a text to a friend with a disturbing and unsettling message. He said that the church would be the first to suffer and that they would get what they deserved after all these years. Mr. F was determined to do what he had to do in order to get back at the church and the people that represented it.

The first murder Mr. F committed was in January. He went to a riverside cottage owned by a retired teacher, Betty Y. Mr. F struck the hapless and frail Betty Y. with her own walking stick four times before he stabbed her. He struck her so hard in the head with the stick that the wood actually splintered. As she lay helpless on the floor, he put a knife deep into the old lady's body. He continued stabbing her for pure pleasure, as the grandmother was already too weak to continue fighting as he plunged his knife into her head and throat. The police later found his footprints all over the old lady's mat.

The second murder took place a month and a half later. He went to Mr. S's vicarage and stabbed him to death with a kitchen knife. During the attack, he kicked the older man down, started yelling at him, and then proceeded to make several deep wound cuts. The Vicar was helpless and could not defend himself in any way. Mr. F went on with the attack until the reverend was dead. Then, Mr. F covered the dead body with porn DVD's, party poppers and condoms. Mr. F put the corpse on the hall floor of the vicarage in front of a mirror that reflected a canvas picture of Jesus and he placed the bible on the victim's chest, laid open to the Letter of Jude, and a picture of a semi-naked model on his lower body. He then spent the night there and watched several Indiana Jones movies and drank beer. Mr. F stole the vicar's phone and started texting all his contacts. Moreover, he sent a text that said: "RIP Mr. S. Pervert" and used his finger to write on the wall the word "help" with blue ink.

Mr. F had planned to crucify the man, but he could not accomplish his whole scheme because he had left behind the bag with hammer and nails. At the vicarage, the police had found, once again, his footprints on the floor.

With forensic evidence, the police found Mr. F to be responsible for both murders. He was caught and arrested on the same month of the second murder. They received a tip from a lady with whom he was staying and the police caught him sneaking out of his house in Folkestone, Kent, at four o'clock in the morning. The police found, among Mr. F's belongings, trousers, a jacket and a knife stained with the vicar's blood.

Mr. F had previously been diagnosed with psychopathic personality disorder. When the police asked him about the murders, he admitted the killing of Mr. S on the grounds of diminished capacity. However, he denied having killed Mrs. Y, although the police later found proof of his guilt in both cases.

A mental health expert told the jury that Mr. F, although he did have a mental disorder, could tell between right and wrong and between what he could or could not do. He chose his actions and was fully aware of what he did and how he did it. Moreover, Mrs. Y's children stated that they were thankful that Mr. F was condemned and out of the streets since they were sure that if he had not been sent to jail, he would have continued to kill more and more innocent people.

As he was officially sentenced in the Bristol Crown Court, Mr. F showed no emotion at all when the judge said he would die in prison as he was sentenced to life, never to be free again. Mr. F stood stonily in his own silence, his face reflecting not an ounce of regret or understanding of the depravity that he had done, all because of his terrible hate for God.

Chapter 8

Nasty Neighbour Blues

In 2008, authorities were called to a house to handle a neighbor dispute. Officer Brown, the officer on the scene, explained that becoming a referee in-between two neighbors with a longstanding feud is a recurring nightmare for police officers' such as himself. When he arrives at the home of the complainant, Officer Brown is greeted by a woman who is completely fed-up with her neighbors. "As an officer, you tend to deal with a lot of people. Therefore, one of the things that gets taken into consideration, as far as the credibility of the complainant is concerned, is their professional behavior and education level. Those that seem to be uneducated and uncivilized are typically not taken very seriously." The cop claims that the woman who greeted him that night when he responded to the call had a very professional demeanor. She seemed normal, well rounded, and there was nothing that would indicate any type of drug abuse or illegal substance-use.

After speaking with her further, he finds out that her neighbors had been making a lot of racial comments directed at her that she found to be very offensive. The neighbors had been yelling through the wall when she was inside her house and she was completely fed-up with this aggressive rudeness and attitude directed at her.

"This... seems legit to me," Officer Brown explained. "She was convincing …. it was always the same story with the same details. In short, I could not twist her story around and say to myself 'seems like bullshit.'"

Convinced that her story was legitimate, he started taking notes on everything that came out of her mouth, which was protocol. She had been living at the address for a little over a month, at that point with her husband. Although she was crazy about her new place, she could not stand her neighbor. Every time she and her husband were in the house, the racist next-door neighbor would shout out : "leave this home!" At this point, she had just had it. After working hard all day, the last thing she wanted to hear was some rude man telling her that she needed to leave.

Continuing on with her story, she told Officer Brown that today was the last straw. She had just got home from the store and was bringing the groceries from her car to the house. To save on time, she wanted to stack all the groceries up by the back door, as opposed to going all the way into the kitchen. While she was rummaging around in the kitchen putting up her things, her neighbor allegedly "shot a 24 case of pop with a pellet gun."

Following protocol, the officer then walks outside to take a look at the case of pop soda that the woman was speaking of. He examined the case and did not find any bullet holes; however, he did notice that several cans inside the case were slowly leaking. What he saw next struck him as strange. "It was also about 70 degrees and beautiful," he explained. So, he opened the case. It was sealed shut and there were four cans that appeared to be smashed up, but the remaining ones looked fine. He did not see any pellet holes or anything else. It was amazing because the way that the cans had been crushed inside the case was almost impossible to accomplish without messing up either the case or the other cans that were inside. "I might be college educated and have some cop experience," he said as he reminisced about the conversation, "but I shrug it off because, how the hell do I know they weren't damaged in packing?" But despite trying to dismiss his suspicions about what had occurred, the officer admitted that his "spider sense started tingling."

Regardless of how the officer felt around that time, he knew that he had to do his job so he went next door to finally meet this trouble-making neighbor that was disturbing the peace. When the door opened, there stood two little old ladies. And not only was it just these two old ladies living inside the neighboring house, but both of them were actually of the same race as the woman who had made the call to complain! There was no basis to the "racist comments" being thrown from the neighboring house directed at the complainant. It was also very clear that there were no adult males staying at that neighboring house with the old ladies. In fact, it did not even look as if any men had been there at all at any time in the recent past

A bit confused, the officer returned to the original neighbor's house to make sure that he went to the correct home. "I go back to my complainant and ask where does the voice come from," he said, "and she points right at the old lady house next door." Still dumbfounded, he asked, was the voice that of a man or a woman. She quickly answered that it was indeed the voice of a male. "He sounds so pissed-off all the time," she added.

The officer was completely confused. On top off that, he was determined to get these two neighbors to cooperate with each other. He did not want to have to go back out there over what seemed to be just a major misunderstanding. He reasoned that whenever you encounter neighbors that you can make happy, they generally do not continue to call the police.

With that in mind, he took the woman next door to meet her "racist neighbors". Only to find out that the complainant had no idea who she had living next door to her all this time. The only encounters she thought she had with the neighbor was when those involved the voice of the racist man. The two old ladies, who were obviously roommates, were so sweet that they even had fresh baked pastries and a tray of candy out for everyone to have for a treat.

Now that everyone was on good terms, the officer started to explain to one of the old ladies why he was there.

"I shit you not" he said, "one looks right at me and goes… 'Bill said that happened to him before he passed.'"

Finally the real story came out that the last person that had lived in the complainant's house was a man named Bill and he had told his next door neighbors, the little old ladies, that there was a man's voice that kept telling him to leave his home. A few months later, the aforementioned Bill, the previous owner, took a handful of sleeping pills and was dead.

As rational as Officer Brown was, he really started to think about all the complaint calls that he had ever received. Crazy or racist neighbors do not yell things such as 'leave the house" he explained, as he continued to rationalize the situation. He goes on to say that typically, a racist would say things that are much more hateful. Only someone or something inside of a home would ever tell you to leave.

The story was never solved with the identity of who it was that was really telling the woman complainant to leave. But a short time later, since the night of her complaint, the woman had a FOR SALE sign posted on her yard and she was packing her truck with her belongings. I guess she wasn't taking any chances with her life while staying in a house with the mysterious voice that no one could explain.

Chapter 9

Everyone Meet Bob

In a small town in Mexico lived a reporter that everyone called Bob D. Bob D was always on the hunt for news, and he frequently listened to police scanners so that he would know about any major police activity in the area. It did not matter whether or not it was a fire breaking out, a massive car wreck holding up track, or anything like that— Bob D was sure to be right there on the scene.

He was definitely no stranger to any of the local officers. In fact, everyone on the force knew who Bob D was because he came around about 1-2 times a week. Bob had a pretty good sense of humor and was often known as being a joker. A lot of times, he would do small things to others to get under their skin like flick them behind the ear. Most of the time, people thought it was just a bug landing on their ear, so they would turn around to see what it was, only to discover that it was just Bob D goofing off. There weren't too many people in the town that didn't care for the guy, he was quite a well-liked fellow. But sadly, Bob D developed lung cancer and ended up dying suddenly. And even though he had requested for his body to be cremated, his wife buried him instead.

Several weeks after the funeral had come and gone, people still spoke about "seeing Bob" in all of the areas that he used to get his top news from car wrecks, fires, etc. Crazily enough, there were about 20-30 different reports like this from both police officers and regular civilians that lived in the area. Despite the high number of people saying that they saw him, the sheriff was not very convinced.

One night, the sheriff showed up at his nephew's house completely terrified. He and his wife came with their guns in, hands and faces as white as paper with sheer horror. When they asked the sheriff what had happened, they had to calm him down first before he could start to tell his story. It was reported that the sheriff was completely frazzled, which was odd, considering the fact that he had never panicked about anything in the past.

He told his nephew that he was in the house watching television with his wife, just like any other day. His ear started itching something crazy, so he started scratching it. His wife, clearly irritated by her husband's movements, asked him what the problem was. The sheriff then turned around just in time to see the door to his bedroom swing open. Standing right there in the doorway, as plain as day, was none other than the famous and recently deceased, Bob D. As you can guess, the sheriff was flabbergasted to see the dead man standing in the middle of his house. He popped up out of his chair and hurried up to get his wife's attention to make sure he wasn't losing his mind. She saw the dead man too and froze. After they both had made contact with the ghost of Bob D, a smile formed across the ghost's face as he turned to walk to the other side of the living room and out through the front of the house. He even made sure to close the door behind him when he left.

As soon as the sheriff was able to shake off his fear and regain control, he ran out the door with his gun ready. He looked around for Bob D, but could not find him. From there, they went straight to his nephew's house. But that night, the sheriff and his wife could not go back to their own home.

The next day when the sheriff got to work, many of the officers were throwing the "we told you so" comments in his face. Strangely enough, that was not the last time that Bob D made his appearance around town. For the next couple of month, others still claimed that he was popping up at police scenes and other newsworthy events. The sheriff's brother even claimed that Bob D had made his way into the dark room of his basement. He wasn't hurting anybody, he was just teasing them by flicking their ears just like he used to do when he was alive.

Sometime during the third month of the town being haunted by the friendly ghost of Bob D, people were saying that the haunt was starting to look less and less like himself. In fact, the sheriff himself said that the two additional times that he saw Bob D again : "he was looking more and more worn." The sheriff's brother made the conjecture that his "wornness" was a result of his actual body decomposing. In other words, the ghost was a reflection of Bob D's true body buried deep in the earth. Bob D was physically gone, but his ghost and the memories he left with the townspeople, made sure that he was never forgotten.

Chapter 10

The Housing Development Site

Jim remembered his first time when he started working as a security guard. One of his strangest first assignments was during the third shift, in a location on the outskirts of town, at a new housing development building. Even though he had only worked there for a short period of time, he claimed that very odd things took place. While Jim was taking care of his regular patrols in the neighborhood, he would see people watching him drive around from the upper windows of the vacant houses. Interestingly enough, by the time he went into one of the houses to investigate, they would be completely deserted.

Jim tried not to think so much about it, and he went on about his daily business. When he arrived on site, Jim liked to go through each of the eight model homes he was assigned to and turn off all the things that generated excess electricity (television, lights, etc.). After the first night, things started to get creepy. As he was going through the kitchen of one of the houses, he heard someone turn off the lights. Well, at least that's what he figured had happened, considering the fact that the breaker wasn't blown or a power surge hadn't occurred.

Not too long after the lights went off, Jim heard another clicking sound and noticed that the lights had gone out in the next house as well. Strangely though, the TV had been left on. Perplexed, Jim went into the house but by the time he got inside, the lights had turned back on and the television had been put on standby mode. Jim noted that the only way that the TV could have been put on standby mode is if the button on the front of the TV set had been touched. He ignored it, and went on to tend to the other houses. Just when he was finishing up with the final house, Jim looked out the window and noticed that both the second and third houses had managed to have their lights turned back on. Again, no one was in the house when he went inside to turn off the lights.

On the third night, the situation involving the lights started to get weirder and weirder. The lights weren't just turning on by themselves when he was in another house. Now, they would do one of two things: flicker on and off in a particular room as soon as he went into one of the houses, or the light that was above the stove would somehow manage to turn itself on. When he would turn to take a closer look at the lights, Jim would hear a whole bunch of clicking sounds coming from the floor above him. It sounded a lot like someone was going through the house turning on all the lights. Being the brave soul that he was, he would then go upstairs to see what was going on. Just as he suspected, most of the lights that he had previously turned off, were now right back on. You would think that this would be enough to make Jim not want to go into any more houses, but he still kept trucking right along as if things were normal, because that was his job as a member of the security force assigned to that location.

When he went into a different house, one of the lamps positioned on the desk kept turning it's switch back on. In fact, it did this three times! In that same house, another lamp that was pretty dim started to light up by itself while Jim was standing right in front of it. If you think this whole experience with the model houses was something, wait until you hear about some of the other scary occurrences that took place while Jim was working nearby the same site.

There was a construction site near the place that he used to patrol. One day as he was going past the site, he saw something that resembled a skunk walk directly behind one of the port-o-potties. Whenever it came back from behind the bathroom, it had transformed from a skunk to a black shi-tzu. If that weren't creepy enough, the thing then continued to transform itself a few more times while it was right there in front of Jim's eyes. The animal literally changed, not only in size, but in color and even shape. It went from a shi-tzu to a Doberman, then a bloodhound and tan mastiff, before finally stopping as it turned into a yellow Labrador Retriever. After it took the shape of the

Lab, it ran off into the dark. Up until that point, Jim had thought that maybe the situation with the lights was just a part of his imagination; however, this transformational beast proved that the place was haunted.

As Jim started walking back towards the front office, he just happened to look up into one of the vacant houses. As soon as he looked up, something hit him on the left side of his body. He's a pretty big guy of about 250 pounds, so it would take a bit of force to sway him. But whatever it was that hit him knocked him heavily off balance. Jim described the feeling as if someone were trying to walk past him and ended up shoving him a bit too hard to get him out of the way. Of course, no one was there, so Jim was terrified. Since that incident, he had politely expressed to his supervisors via a formal request, his decision to decline ever being assigned to patrol that site again.

Chapter 11

The Abandoned Hospital

A little while before Brandon joined the police force, he recalls working for a hospital as one of the security guards. The job was perfect except for the fact that during graveyard shift hours, he was all by himself. On top of that, the hospital was completely abandoned during that time.

A year before he started working there, the hospital had constructed a brand-new building that had replaced the one that had been built in the 1900s. The building was fairly large, standing about five floors high. Once the hospital was cleared out, all of the patients, doctors, and nurses left. They didn't tidy anything up on their way out. All of their tools and supplies were left right in place, as if they were trying to leave in a rush. Everything was still there, from the half empty coffee mugs, wheel chairs sitting around in odd places, and even uniforms still tucked neatly away on a rack. Everything was still there, just collecting dust.

Brandon had always enjoyed working the graveyard shift because he didn't really scare easily. Every night that he had to work, he would make his way through the halls. Usually, he would walk but every now and then, he would ride in a wheel chair since he was alone and the building was supposed to be empty and unused. For some reason, he would have to keep re-locking and closing certain doors. He would start on the first floor, and then make his way up to the remaining four floors every night.

He didn't begin to get nervous until about an hour after he had walked down the hallway to turn off lights and do patrol. This was because he had to close the exact same doors and cut off the same lights that he had already done on his first round there. Another thing that would happen is that he would be going down a hall and then all of a sudden he would hear footsteps on the floor that was directly above him. He would then also start hearing different doors opening and closing. The elevators would start to move from floor to floor without him touching any of the controls, the phones would start ringing out of nowhere, and even the nurse call lights would start blinking.

Despite everything that was going on, Brandon stated that "there were only three times that I got the 'I hate this shit' feeling". The first time he got the feeling was when he had been checking the offices on the fourth floor of the hospital. One of the lights was on in the locked hallway, for some reason. Brandon knew it didn't make sense for the light to be on because the hallway hadn't gone through any renovations since it was originally built in the 1900's when electricity wasn't even used in the hospital yet, back in the olden days of the original structure. Nevertheless, he went to unlock the door, turn off the lights, leave the hallway, and relock the same door. As he was about to leave, he heard the sound of the light switch. Peering through the frosted glass, he saw that the light had turned itself back on. Terrified, he decided not to go back to the hallway during the remainder of the night.

The second time that Brandon had a creepy experience was when he was riding the elevator back and forth between floors. As he was taking the elevator to the fifth floor, he heard the sound of laughter and talking. The higher the elevator went, the louder the voices sounded. As soon as he got to the top floor, all the noises completely stopped. Every single light on that floor had been turned on, including the patient rooms. Brandon was stunned because he knew for sure that he had heard voices. Determined to find out who it was, he says he "checked high and low. . . . and there was not a single living and breathing person in that place except for me."

The worst encounter came on the third night. It started off as being a normal, average night. Brandon was on the first floor, locking all the doors in the corridor. This particular door had glass in the center, but the back of it was covered with a few strips of white tape. The room that the glass door led to was pretty dark, and the hallway that was close to Brandon had a dim light shining through it. The glass was a perfect mirror to see behind him. Everything was normal until he looked up and saw a full outline of a person walk past him. There was no denying what Brandon saw. "Clear as day," he explained, "just a full shadow of a person walked past." He claimed that he was petrified with fear for a minute before he ran after the person that he thought he saw. When he went after it, it had completely disappeared,

Although he enjoyed his time at the hospital, Brandon was already quite scared with all his unexplained experiences. Other guards that worked on different days also came back with similar stories. They claimed that most of the same things occurred, with the exception being that they always saw shadowy nuns walk around into the patient rooms on the 3rd floor.

Chapter 12

The Keyholder

Two police officers were called to go check out an alarm that had gone off nearby. When they got to the location, they pulled up in front of an aged office building that had been renovated into doctor's offices. The building had a pharmacy that was attached to it on one side. The reason the police officers were here was because the local dispatch had received a motion signal from one of the offices upstairs. The person who had the key to the building came to the location, and then the officers proceeded to secure the perimeter. Unfortunately, the key holder did not have keys to the stairs that were locked behind the door, so the officers took the elevator up to the floor where the motion detector went off.

The elevator went to the second floor and opened up to a dark hallway. The only light was coming from an overhead fixture at the very end of the hall. Following protocol, the officers began to check all of the doors. As far as they could tell, thus far, everything seemed to be secured. Once they got to the last office at the end of the hallway, the door was unlocked. Proceeding with caution, they entered the room. After looking around, they reached the conclusion that the office space was not being used. They opened another and saw a large waiting room and a reception area. It contained 10-12 examination rooms that were all cleared with no mishaps. Everything seemed okay, so they proceeded to leave.

As the officers were leaving the office, something just did not seem right to them. At that point, one of the officers realized that the dim light that had previously lit their way the first time was now completely turned off. Now, another light was on that was closer to the elevators. The officer who was giving his account of what he saw next, then stated that: "I looked at my squad mate and saw that he was completely white. I asked him what was wrong and he replied with a question. He asked if all the doors we had just checked were closed and locked. When I told him yes, he said that they were now standing wide open." Oddly enough, every single door that they had just spent the last few minutes testing were now flung completely open. Both officers were terrified.

But because they had a job to do, they continued to secure, check and clear each of the offices. Everything seemed to be okay as they finished up with the last office. As they were on their way out through the door and about to turn around the corner to go to the waiting area, the main door slams completely shut. And all of a sudden, both of their radios start making strange noises with a lot of static feedback. "Now I just wanted to get the hell out of there" the officer adds.

The two officers hurry back to the elevator and head down to the first floor. They had to get in contact with the key holder one more time before they left the premises. For some reason, the key holder was nowhere to be found. The officers attempted to make contact with their dispatch so that they could request a call back number for the key holder. They had to let him know what they had found. The dispatch let them know that the key holder was on her way and should be there within the next five minutes. Confused, they told their dispatch they had already been in contact with the key holder earlier on in the night.

The dispatch then stated that it was impossible for the officers to have talked with the key holder because the alarm company had only just contacted one. When the real key holder showed up in person, she asked about the person that had let them into the building claiming to be the authorized key holder. The woman stated that the officers' description of the man matched that of a doctor that used to work on the second floor of the same building that they had just searched. Ironically, the man had committed suicide in his home a few days prior to the incident. To this day, the two officers still have no idea how this dead man was able to let them into the building. The two officers have also never returned to that haunted office building, or it's perimeter ever again.

Chapter 13

The Church That Was Haunted

Grant used to have a job working for a private police/security firm. His official title was a patrol supervisor. He had a lot of routes, and one of these included a really big church that also had a private day care and kindergarten attached to it. The biggest responsibility that Grant had to fulfill was to make sure that the building was secure and clear every evening from 3 a.m.- 4 a.m. The reason it was so important was because there had been recent instances in which a lot of the doors to the building were left open in the morning.

Back in the early 1900's, the old building had been a small schoolhouse. The story goes that the school somehow managed to catch fire, killing all of the children that had been trapped inside. Prior to working for the company, no one had told this to Grant. Sadly, after only one week of being there, Grant had requested the church to be either removed from his route or scheduled to be earlier from the timeslot of the 3 a.m – 4 a.m. shift. This was because while he was assigned to patrol the church, several unexplainable things happened.

Grant talked about some of the details from his very first night on his church patrol on the job. He had just walked down a very long hallway where all of the main classrooms were located, in order to clear out and check on all of the rooms. When Grant turned to walk back up the hallway, he saw that there was a red balloon randomly floating down the middle of the hallway that he knew was definitely not there before. While seeing a red balloon in mid-air may not seem like the creepiest thing that could occur to an officer, Grant was officially spooked at that point with the balloon's random appearance on that night, at that very strange moment.

On another evening, he recalled an incident that took place inside the office of the pastor. Inside, there was a lighthouse-shaped lamp that rested on a table, directly facing a huge window. Every time Grant pulled up to the church, he would see the lamp clear as day in the front of the office window. There was never a time when the lamp was not on when he drove up. Interestingly enough, once he would go inside to go check on the pastor's office and lock everything up, the lamp would mysteriously be turned off. By the time he was done and back in his car to get ready to leave after his shift, the light would be on again.

Another weekend, the church was putting together a bake sale. As you can imagine, the church's kitchen was stocked full of sweets including plates of cookies, cakes, brownies, etc. Someone had left a note on the back door letting the security know that they were more than welcome to help themselves to the snacks that were in the kitchen. Grant made his way into the kitchen to clean everything up. He happened to notice a big plate of fresh chocolate chip cookies sitting on the counter. Ignoring the plate, he went to clear the remainder of the kitchen. As he went back to the counter to get the plate of chocolate chip cookies, there were several cookies missing. In fact, there were only three left when there had been at least twelve before he walked away.

Grant also dealt with doors that he had already closed or locked, mysteriously opening and unlocking themselves without anyone else being around. Other officers had similar unexplainable encounters at this church. In fact, the officer that took Grant's place one night quit the job the very next day. His reason? When he was investigating the chapel, the pipe organ began to play a song all on it's own with no one around.

Chapter 14

The Children in The Attic

Trevor was out for his normal patrol on a late Nebraska winter night. The ground was covered in snow, and nothing seemed to be out of the normal. There were several areas in the Nebraska town that were peppered with abandoned houses. Due to the rising price of copper, the police had also seen a rise in copper theft from old plumbing in the abandoned homes. Regular patrols were necessary in order to keep thieves from stealing these costly pipes.

On this particular evening, Trevor did his normal drive through one particular abandoned area. He drove past one of the homes at around eight that night, and everything looked as normal as it should be. The house was on a corner, so the officer was able to see all four sides of the house as he drove around. He continued his patrol to other areas.

About two hours later, Trevor looped back around to do another pass through that particular street since he knew the corner lot was abandoned. As he passed by, he noticed the back door of the house was wide open, something he knew had to have happened in the two-hour period since he drove through the area. From his car, he didn't see any sign of intruders, including footprints that should have been around the door area. He called into the station to let them know he would be checking out the house and parked his car.

The wintry night air added to the already uneasy feeling Trevor had as he approached the abandoned home. He took a walk around the perimeter but still didn't find any sign of footprints, so he went back to the open door. As he stepped inside, he noticed the house was completely empty and it had obviously been gutted. He looked down as his boots scraped across the dusty floor realizing there were no footprints in the dirt either.

The officer shines his flashlight around the room, but all he sees is torn down walls and piles of plaster in different places. He takes one last look at the floor for any sign of footprints and shrugs. With no evidence of intrusion, he chalks it up to the wind or a loose lock on the door. He turns to walk out when he hears a large thump coming from upstairs. He pauses for a moment, and the thump is followed by the sound of children laughing. He calls out to the kids, telling them to come down immediately.

"This is the police, come downstairs."

The house fell silent, so Trevor radioed in possible intruders and made his way through the house to the back staircase that leads upstairs. He walked slowly looking for any footprints he might have missed, pausing a couple more times at the sound of children playing upstairs. When no one responded, he started to think his hearing was skewed and he would find nothing more than an animal or an open window upstairs. Slowly he climbed the creaky staircase, his flashlight as the only source of light in the house.

When the officer reached the top of the stairs, he paused and notices three bedrooms, one to the right, one to the left, and one straight ahead. All the doors are shut, and he hears nothing but the wind outside. He steps forward and turns to the right but stops at the sound of another thump coming from the bedroom to his left. He walks slowly to the door and turns the handle to the bedroom. As the door swings open, he shines his flashlight in, looking quickly around the room.

It's empty except for a small pile of dirt and plaster in the middle of the floor. He turns to walk away when a piece of paper placed gingerly at the top of the pile catches his eye. He walks over to the pile and peers down at the paper. Sounds of children's laughter echo quietly through the hallway as he picks up the page ripped from a long-ago children's book. On the torn-out page is a photo of a police officer.

The officer reports that he dropped the torn paper, checked the other rooms quickly and left as fast as possible. There wasn't a living soul in the house that night.

He never went back.

Chapter 15

Revelations of a Victim

It was Chris's second year on patrol and his night started like any other. Chris and his partner collected their patrol route for the evening and set out. About an hour into the ride, a call came over the radio concerning a man that was holding a gun to a woman's head. The two immediately took the call and raced over, lights and sirens flashing.

When the Officers arrived, they came face to face with a very upset, and very frantic woman. She was shaking and crying and would say nothing more than, "He shot me in the head," over and over again. The police did a search of the premises but found no one else there. They continued to tell the woman that she was okay and that no one had shot her. Once she calmed down a bit, they asked if she had family or friends close by that they could call, but she shook her head no. Finally, after she agreed that she would be okay if they left, the Officers left the scene.

The Officers were slightly shaken but assumed the woman had some sort of mental instability and finished their patrol with no other calls. When they arrived back at the precinct, they told their Sergeant about the strange call and the frantic woman. The other officers thought it was weird as well, so they looked the woman up in their database. As the pages of their search flashed on the screen, the whole of the police precinct went quiet and the men turned white as ghosts.

From the description in their system, this exact woman had been shot in the head by her husband one year ago to the date. The husband was never caught, and the case was still under investigation. The police officers didn't believe what they just saw, assuming they had gotten her name wrong or someone was playing a bad joke and so the officers put the encounter behind them. As time went by, Chris, the first police officer, completely forgot about the incident.

Several years later, Chris was in charge of training for one of the new recruits in the precinct. They met at the station and picked up their route for the night watch in town. Everything was quiet that night, and Chris even mentioned that it was eerily still outside. His town didn't see a lot of crime, but there were at least some misbehaving teenagers, or a domestic dispute or two to handle on a regular basis.

As the two drove through their route, they noticed that most of the lights on the light poles were flickering in and out and that there didn't seem to be any trace of people out, especially in the more crowded areas of town. He shook it off, blaming the weather or the time of year, but something didn't quite sit well with him.

After several hours of driving with no calls, and no one to pull over, the radio started crackling and then a call came through loud and clear. There was a woman who had called 911, and she was frantically crying, explaining that her husband was trying to kill her. Chris and his new recruit on the police force took the call immediately, and Chris didn't think anything of it until he began to pull up to the house he had been at years before. As they approached, the same woman he had calmed down in that same yard years before, was standing, crying in the street.

Chris pulled up to the house, and then looked down at the radio as it continued to crackle and break up louder and louder. He stepped out of his car and walked towards the crying woman. He asked if she were okay, but she said nothing. She pulled her hands from her face and pointed at the house. He looked up to see the door cracked open and a light coming from inside. As he grew closer and closer, he realized that this wasn't someone telling him of recent physical abuse, this was someone pointing out her own murderer.

Lo and behold, when the police officers entered the house, they found the dead woman's husband inside. He had come back into town and stopped at his house. The same house he had shot his wife in, years before. They arrested him, and he was later charged with murder. After that moment, Chris never heard from or saw the women again. He assumed that she had finally found her peace but that didn't stop the eerie feeling he would always have since that time, whenever the night was calm, and his police radio would begin to crackle.

Chapter 16

The Little Girl

Everybody hated the storms in the Western part of Nebraska, especially Joe, the on-duty cop that constantly found himself outside dealing with one thing or another. It was a normal wet night when Joe started his night-shift rounds. Nothing much usually happened out there late at night, and Joe was looking forward to a quiet patrol. It had been about two hours into the evening shift when a call came over the radio. An older lady lived alone in a farmhouse on the edge of town and called in a report of a young girl running around her backyard.

Joe sighed as he switched on his wipers and headed towards the house, knowing for sure he'd end up drenched after this call. As he pulled into the long driveway, goosebumps suddenly ran up his arms, and he braked slightly as a thick mist floated across the driveway. Between the old creaky shutters and the worn roof, this house looked like something straight out of a horror movie. Joe flinched slightly as he put the car in park and watched the lightning flash across the sky. He ran up to the porch and shook the water from his hat before approaching the front door. Just as a clap of thunder shook across the Nebraska sky, the elderly woman opened the door and took a peek out at the officer. A look of relief washed over her when she realized who he was, and she quickly opened the door to invite him in. Joe looked around the dusty old house and realized the lady must be living there alone. She looked a little scared, but in this kind of storm, it was hard not to be.

The lady explained that she had seen a little girl running around the backyard, in and out of the trees that peppered the field behind the house. Joe walked over to the back sliding door and looked out into the darkness. With the clouds covering the moon, the yard was pitch black, but even with the flashes of lightning lighting up the field, he didn't see any signs of anyone. He cracked the door open and shined his flashlight around the yard, but still no sign. He was about to step out when he heard a gasp from behind him.

"She's there," the old lady yelled. "She's in the house."

Joe turned quickly around and caught the back of a pink flowered dress disappear around the corner. How had she gotten past him so quickly and why wasn't she wet? Joe jogged around the corner as the young girl turned around, an eerie giggle floating through the air. Then, without warning, she disappeared right in front of his eyes. He rubbed his face not sure of what just happened when the old lady yelled out again.

"There," she pointed. "She's outside again."

Joe ran over to the door and watched as the little girl skipped out into the field and disappeared into the fog. He pulled the hood of his rain jacket over his head and headed out into the field. Joe searched for several hours but found no trace of the little girl anywhere. After showing the woman that she had been left alone and there was nobody there and finally getting her calmed down, Joe went back to the police precinct, dumbfounded by what had happened.

Months went by with no word, and after the old lady had passed, a new family moved into the old farmhouse on the edge of town. One stormy night Joe came on duty and found that a call had come in from the same house talking about the same little girl appearing inside their home. This time, though, he passed the call to someone else, still unable to shake the eerie feeling of that thick fog rolling across the driveway.

Chapter 17

Shadows and Cameras

Tony was used to his fair share of ghost stories growing up, and eventually he became a police officer in Salem, Massachusetts. With the city's historical reverence and rich ancestral connection with witchcraft, you begin to become kind of numb to it. When Tony was a rookie, the guys used to tell him all kinds of stories before sending him out on patrol by himself. But nothing ever happened.

Nothing that is, until he started receiving patrols on the outskirts of the city. About ten years prior, there had been some uproar about ritual sacrifices and ghostly apparitions haunting the residents, but Tony didn't believe any of it to be true. He took his shift like every other night and headed over to the west outskirts. The night was dark, and though the moon was giving off some light, the eerie shadows that crept through the neighborhood almost felt like they were taking on a life of their own. The first night Tony began to be spooked, he was parked in the back of a neighborhood, finishing up paperwork from that night's patrol when he heard a strange noise by his car.

Tony flipped on the exterior lights and looked around but didn't see anything and chalked it up to some sort of wild animal like a raccoon. He continued filling out his paperwork when the sound came again, this time much louder and quicker than any animal he knew of. So, in order to assess any damage and find the perpetrator, Tony got out of his vehicle and called out, but to no avail. The air was silent and still and there was no sign of foot, or paw, prints anywhere near his car. Tony turned to get back in the car assuming the animal had run off when the driver's side door slammed shut. He pulled his weapon and shined the light into the car, but there was no one inside. He felt a bit uneasy but shrugged it off and finished his shift.

The next night Tony was assigned to the same section of town, and it was pretty quiet except for some random calls about someone seeing the shadow of a person walking through their backyard. Tony went to the call and talked to the homeowner. They had been sitting in their living room when a shadow fell over them from the back door. When they turned to look, no one was there. They ignored it the first couple of times but then called the police, worried someone was planning on breaking into the house. Tony checked the yard and the perimeter for any sign of intruders but didn't see anyone. He decided to finish up his paperwork parked outside of their house just to make sure.

As Tony sat in his car typing away on his laptop, a shadow fell over him, and he looked out expecting to see someone standing beside the driver's side door, but when he looked no one was there. He continued working when he heard a strange noise and looked out at the house to see what it was. To his relief, it was just a cat in the garbage can. However, as he chuckled to himself and turned to look back down at his laptop, something caught his eye. The shadow of a person emerged from behind a tree and moved from the passenger side of the car, across the hood and to the driver's side. Just as Tony was about to get out, he heard a loud pop and the window in his cruiser smashed in. There was no sign of anyone, anywhere.

Thinking he must have caught the perp on his dash cam, he pulled images up on his phone. He watched as the shadow, not connected to anyone, moved to the front of the car and then as if someone put their finger over the lens, it went black for a few moments. When the obstruction moved from the camera, it was showing directly after the window was smashed. This freaked Tony out something awful, and after showing his Sergeant, he requested never to be put on that watch again. The precinct received several calls about the mysterious shadow after that, but Tony decided to stick with witches instead of ghouls.

Chapter 18

The Red Ribbon

The children's hospital in the center of the old factory business had been there for several decades. It was upgraded each year but had cared for sick children even during the Great Depression. Some of the most pronounced Pediatric Cancer Research was performed there, and it was hub and center of their little Oklahoma town. Because the hospital brought in so much news and travel from other places, the city made sure that public tax dollars were spent keeping the place updated and safe.

The Mayor had organized an alliance between the City's Police Department and the hospital to help bring security in throughout the day and night at the ward. The town wasn't dangerous but it being a hospital, they had their fair share of people wandering in off the street. The children in the hospital suffered from all different sorts of illnesses, but they were well taken care of.

In this small town, during the great depression, those children who were suffering from terminal illnesses had red ribbons tied to the ends of their beds so that if an evacuation occurred, they knew who needed special care during transport. Back then, however, many of the diseases that are curable now were life-ending diseases back then. The hospital, due to the past use of red ribbons for terminal patients, stayed away from the use of ribbon for any reason in the current day practice. They were thought to hold negative energy, something none of the children needed.

Recently, due to an enormous Federal Grant, the hospital had undergone enormous renovations. All of the children in the Cancer Ward were moved down a floor, and the area was closed. At night, it was quiet upstairs since construction would disturb the kids when they were supposed to be resting. The staff worried that children or intruders could enter in through the back area and hide out in the renovated areas during the night, so the police department sent an officer over to patrol the floors.

Avery was relatively new to the force, having come from the Boston PD, but looking for a calmer, less stressful way of life. He loved kids and was more than happy to take the night watch at the hospital. Each evening he would visit with the kids before heading upstairs to keep watch. He was about a week into the watch when things started to feel a bit strange upstairs. As the renovations continued, the construction workers would often find old remnants of the hospital from the past and leave them sitting around to be collected with the rest of the trash. Avery found the old stuffed animals and surgical gear to be a bit spooky.

On the night in question, Avery had done two circles around the closed floor and had turned the corner to clear the rest of the rooms when he heard small steps running down the hallway. He turned and shined his flashlight, but didn't see anything, not even footprints in the dust. He shrugged it off and continued to work. As he exited one of the rooms, he heard the sound of giggling across the hall. Assuming one of the children had followed him up, he walked in laughing, trying not to scare them. However, when he got in the room, there was no one there.

He went back out and made his way towards the exit, ready to grab a cup of coffee and take a break. As he reached the stairwell, he heard a door shut, so he quickly turned around and stared down the hallway. He looked up, noticing movement, and in the center of the hall was a small red ribbon floating in the air. Avery backed out of the floor and told the nurse, who was more than spooked. The next day Avery asked to be taken off the watch. He knew the children meant him no harm, but just the thought of those lost souls wandering around the renovated floor shook him to the core.

Chapter 19

Dark Shadows

When you hear the word California, immediately sand, surf, sun, and bikinis come to mind. But as you drive North, away from the glam and glitz of celebrity homes, and reach the point where the ocean breeze no longer cools the hot sun of summer, you reach the deserts. Summer days seem to go on forever, and the clear, treeless plains of sand do little to provide shelter from the smoldering sun overhead.

These deserts are home to a rich cultural divide, where the hills come alive with Native American Culture. Much of the land provided by the government to the tribes reside in these hot desert areas. Growing crops are pretty much out of the question, so many times Casinos are an excellent way to draw in the white man, and make a living while maintaining cultural heritage. Unfortunately, with so much greed breeding throughout the country, parcels of land have been taken back from the Native Americans and handed over to greedy white businessmen who build Casinos as a way to drive out the cultural inertia of the Native Americans and cash in on the tourist dollar.

In the late 2000's a large parcel of land was seized by the government and sold to the highest bidder. The tribes attempted to stop the sale, showing ample evidence of cultural artifacts and Native burial sites located in the middle of the property. However, the government, their eyes fixated on the green, ignored their requests and handed the keys to a rich oil tycoon who was ready to try his hand at Casinos. Protests raged as the Casino was being built, but after a while, they died out, the local Native Americans realizing the damage had been done.

However, just a few years later, that same businessman grew greedier and decided that it was time to expand his empire to the untouched portion of his stolen land. This untouched portion just happened to be exactly where the burial grounds were located. When the locals caught wind of the new plan, protests erupted once again, oftentimes becoming violent. In order to protect both sides of the issue, police were scheduled to do watches throughout the days and nights, to make sure that neither side came to a violent end.

Lonnie had lived in the area his whole life but knew little about the local culture. He was assigned the rove watch at the Casino on third shift, a shift he was more than happy to take since the nights were cool, sometimes even cold, in the California desert.

The lights from the front of the Casino tended to cast deep shadows around the back, but Lonnie enjoyed the quiet of the desert, so he spent much of his time watching around the rear entrance. Several times throughout the night he stopped, swearing he saw the dark shadows of people standing on the top railings near the roof and looking out over the hills. However, when he would get closer, the shadows would disappear. Lonnie brought it up to one of the other officers, but he joked around saying they were the ancient spirits from the burial grounds.

Later in the week, during one of Lonnie's routine shifts, he noticed a rise in protests out front and found that in the next day or two the company would be bulldozing the area said to be an ancient Native American cemetery. Though the people were angry, the protests mostly consisted of prayer and song, and the enchanting melody of the people of the desert floated through the night, calming some of Lonnie's anxiety.

As the protestors began to fade away, Lonnie went around back for one last walk through before the sun breached the horizon. He stopped half way across the walk when he noticed several shadowed figures standing on the balcony, looking out over the hills below. He yelled out to them, but they did not move. He took a couple steps further and told them to come down immediately and that it was unlawful for them to be on the property.

With those words, the black shadowy figure on the end turned towards Lonnie and stepped off the balcony. He watched as the shadow hit the ground and stood just several yards away, staring directly at him. Though still a shadow, he thought he could make out the face of an older Native American Man. As Lonnie stepped closer the shadow took flight, a high-pitched scream echoing from its mouth. The figure floated faster and faster towards Lonnie before colliding with him and knocking him backward onto the ground.

When he came to, there were several people talking about what they saw. Apparently, the scream had been heard all across the Casino. The last thing imprinted in Lonnie's mind, though, was the face of an angry Native American man heading directly for him. They never shut down the casino, and even, reportedly continued with their plans of extraction. After a shadowy attack like that, however, Lonnie was happy to move to a new assignment. He hasn't been back since.

Chapter 20

Vanishing Calls

Police departments, in general, tend to get calls on a regular basis that end up being nothing more than a waste of everyone's time. Whether they are a false alarm or a prank call, officers have to walk into it with the belief that every call is sincere. Officer Ellijah knows all too well about taking calls seriously after a course of events in his past that not only led him to discover something gruesome, but may have also freed a soul from an eternity of endless suffering.

Growing up in rural Minnesota, Ellijah passed the old farmhouse on River Road almost every day. The people that lived there seemed pretty quiet and kept to themselves. Because of the dilapidated state of the house, and the secretive nature of the people who lived there, Ellijah heard all kinds of creepy stories about the place. When Ellijah was leaving for the Police Academy, he noticed that whoever had lived there seemed to have just vanished. The place looked completely vacant, and no one ever saw the lady of the house again. He assumed the people had moved.

Fast forward to about ten years later, and Ellijah had just gotten on duty at the local station and was filling out some paperwork. It was the late shift, so not many officers were on duty. Ellijah, though a detective, tended to take the routine calls when he worked that late. Around 11 pm a call came in from a lady who was crying and hard to understand. Ellijah attempted to calm the woman down so he could get her information since the call came in as Unknown. Suddenly, the woman gasps and the call drops. Ellijah traces the call, and the address comes up on River Road. He doesn't connect it to the farmhouse right away since there are several houses on that street.

He makes his way to River Road and pulls up in front of the old farmhouse. There are no lights on, and the place looks completely abandoned. He gets out and does a perimeter check before knocking on the front door. He stands there for several minutes listening but hears nothing. The last knock was pretty hard, and the door creaked open. He called out to anyone that might be inside and began to search the house. The electricity didn't work, and it was obvious, from the lack of any furniture and the collected piles of dust and debris, that no one had lived there for a long time. He finally found the telephone connect in the kitchen, but there was no power, much less any phone connected to it.

Fearing the system gave him the wrong address Ellijah checked with all the houses on the block, but no one had made any kind of call. Feeling he had done his due diligence, Ellijah went back to the precinct and finished out his night. When it came time for shift change, as he was gathering his things, the same call came in. He told the officers he had gone out that night, and there was no one in the house. They told him they had gone out there over a dozen times that week, but someone kept calling. He shrugged and wished them good luck and went home.

The next night Ellijah showed up for work, but this time he was happy to have someone to talk to since his partner was on duty with him that night. The phones were quiet most of the night until about 11 pm. Ellijah's partner picked up the phone and began trying to calm someone down. He shrugged and hit the speaker button so Ellijah could hear. It was the same lady, and as the call had gone the night before, she gasps and then the line disconnects. The two, due to precinct regulations, were obligated to go check it out. They fully expected to pull up in front of the old empty house and find nothing, but this wasn't the case this time.

Standing in the front yard was a small middle-aged woman, crying, with her arms wrapped around her waist. The officers attempted to talk to her, but all she did was wave them to follow her inside. Though it wasn't customary to walk into a house not knowing what to expect, the officers found no other alternative. The woman walked them through the quiet, empty house, and down into the cellar. She turned to them and pointed to a large trunk in the corner. The two officers pried the box open and stood back, realizing there were bones of a person inside the trunk. They quickly turned around to question the woman, but she was gone.

Ellijah's partner called in the finding while Ellijah ran up the stairs, searching the house for the lady, but she had just vanished. His partner called him downstairs on the radio, and he went down to see what he had found.

"There are no footprints," his partner said pointing at the dusty floor. "She didn't have shoes on, there would be footprints."

The two officers logged and assisted the crime scene lab with the discovery. The bones were sent for identification, and after about three months Ellijah had all but forgotten about the case. One day, the lab called and told him they had I.D.'d the River Road Jane Doe found in the basement. They sent the information over. As Ellijah read the report and scrolled down to the picture of the woman, his skin went pale and he called his partner over. His partner looked at the picture on the screen not knowing what he was looking at.

"Oh, hey, man, that's the lady from the house," he said chuckling. "Guess she does exist."

Ellijah grabbed his arm before he could walk away and scrolled up a bit. The woman that had been I.D.'d as the dead body was the woman that led them to the bones. They never got another call, but the house still sits eerily vacant at the end of River Road.

Chapter 21

Crime Scene Photos

Tara had been the local Crime Scene Photographer for over ten years and had seen some pretty gruesome stuff. Though it was often hard for people to be in these crime scenes, Tara found that looking through the lens of her camera was a really good way to pinpoint evidence that may have otherwise been missed. She had seen gruesome deaths, malpractice within hospitals, car accidents, plane accidents, you name it. She was so used to the blood and gore that her coworkers at the precinct always tried to ruffle her feathers. But there was no scaring Tara.

One evening she got the call of a double homicide but was warned that she needed to take pictures while the bodies were still in there. There was a mother and child that were murdered, gruesomely, and they needed as much evidence intact that they could find. Tara didn't get spooked, but she hated being the photographer that had to document the bodies. It always seemed so impersonal and uncomfortable to her, especially when there were children involved.

She arrived quickly at the old warehouse apartment building and made her way to the top floor. The apartment had been renovated, and the living room had floor to ceiling windows. She quickly took pictures of all of the positioning of the bodies and the material around them. Tara would have to stay and retake all the pictures once the bodies were cleared so when she was done, she walked outside for some fresh air and a cup of coffee. As she made her way down the service stairs, she couldn't help but feel a bit uncomfortable, almost as if someone was walking with her, but she was the only one there. She shook it off and chalked it up to just having taken pictures of a dead child.

However, there was a feeling in her chest she couldn't seem to shake, and she stopped momentarily at the bottom of the stairs. Her emotions were all over the place, and she felt so angry. After ten years of taking photos, Tara had never felt such strong emotion but the weird part was, she didn't know why she was so upset. As soon as she stepped out of the doors and into the fresh air, the feeling lifted, and Tara waited until she could go back in and finish up the job.

Once the coroner had completed moving the bodies, Tara went back upstairs and started snapping all the photos. She usually asked the room be cleared of staff so that she didn't miss anything. As she stood in the cold apartment snapping pictures of the blood smeared floors, that emotion came back to her, and the hairs on the back of her neck stood up. With every flash of the camera, the emotions seemed to intensify until Tara had to stop and take a deep breath. The officers on the scene made sure she was okay and joked that someone was haunting her. She didn't seem to find anything funny at that time. She hurried up and finished taking the photos and headed out of the building. Just as before, as soon as she stepped out of the front door the feeling lifted immediately.

Back at the station, she started printing the photos and going through each one. She was tired, and there were several hundred pictures, so she put them into piles. As she went to grab one pile, she looked down at the photo she had taken of the picture window with the bloody handprints. Not believing what she was seeing, she went and flipped on the main light to the conference room and started spreading the pictures out so she could have a better look. Tara put her hand to her chest, a feeling of sadness spreading over her.

In every picture of the window, there was the victim, holding her child, standing behind Tara in the reflection. Though Tara felt sadness, the victim's face was pure rage and as the flashes went off Tara could see the woman screaming in anger behind her. There had been a very violent crime in that apartment, and the ghosts that remained were so angry, they showed up in Tara's photos. She took the photos to her chief and told him someone else would have to follow up.

Chapter 21

The Swamp

In the 1950's in a rural area of southern Louisiana, a plane carrying over 200 people mysteriously crashed into the swamplands below. The crash was so violent that no bodies were recovered, and if anything had been left intact, the swamp gators got to them before the crews could get in to recover. Since the technology wasn't as it was in today's society, and the crash left little evidence behind, the authorities never found out what happened on that warm summer night. The deaths of those killed in the crash were memorialized years later with a statue on the side of the road by the swamp.

As with every other violent event that happens, rumors and stories spread through time, claiming ghosts and apparitions haunt that vacant swampland. After so many years, the only remnants of the crash that can be found is the commemoration. Otherwise, the swamp has taken over all evidence of the plane crash, and ecology has blossomed where before it was once all charred and burnt. Many people, especially the older folks who remember the horrific incident, refuse to go down that road, especially at night. Reports of cries and walking apparitions have been reported at the scene of the accident, especially on the Anniversary of the Incident.

Nialle had moved to Louisiana from California after accepting a position with their police force. He was an extreme skeptic when it came to anything paranormal and had to stifle his amusement when he heard stories of the ghosts that walked the swamp. The area, in his opinion, was the perfect place to catch speeders, and DUI's, especially on the weekend. It was a back road, and people think they can speed through without paying attention. The other officers warned Nialle about the legends, but he laughed it off, figuring they were just trying to freak him out so they could snag his spot.

For days Nialle sat in that exact spot, nabbing speeder after speeder that came down the road. Sometimes he would be so busy that he would stay parked in front of the monument for his entire shift. A few days later, the Chief asked Nialle to knock out the night shift, hoping they could curb the DUI fatality rate on that specific road. Nialle agreed, liking the solace of working the overnight.

When his shift started, he pulled into his regular spot and set up his radar. The bars hadn't let out yet, so the road was quiet and the sounds of frogs were the only thing moving in the swamp behind him. As he typed on his computer, catching up on paperwork, he heard a small thump outside of the car. He stopped for a moment and listened, ultimately going back to his work figuring it was just a gator in the swamp. A few moments later the sound of scratching moved from the passenger side of the car down to the truck and stopped.

Nialle, aware of the creatures that lurked around those parts, grabbed his battalion and weapon and opened the door, checking under the car before putting his feet down. He walked around the car, shining his light on the ground and around the swamp. There was no sign of anything in the area. He leaned down and looked at the marks on the side of the car and rubbed it with his finger. There seemed to be some kind of ash or dust in two long streaks that ran down to the bumper and stopped. At that moment, a breeze ran through the swamp sending chills up his neck. He laughed it off, got back in his car and carried on with his work.

The next night he followed the same routine, and about two hours after sitting there, he heard the same noise, but this time it was louder. He jumped out of the car and looked around, seeing nothing but some jumping frogs. He walked around to the side of the car to find even more black soot smeared across the passenger side. He took in a deep breath, the smell of fuel and something burning stinging his nose. He looked around, thinking something might be on fire, but there was no sign of anything anywhere. He thought about the stories he had been told where people smelled the burning fuel of the plane that night but laughed at himself for even entertaining the idea.

The next night, his last night of evening patrol, he sat comfortably in his car watching the road for speeders. Around the same time as the previous nights, he began to hear the sound of scratching on his car. He jumped out of the vehicle and called out. Everything was silent, but the smell of burning fuel began wafting through the air. He bent down and inspected the mark on his car. This time, though, it started with a small handprint. He stood up quickly and looked around, the hair on the back of his neck standing straight up. The frogs had silenced themselves, and Nialle could hear what sounded like crying. The crying grew louder and as it did more cries joined in until it sounded almost like a stadium of people. He looked around, panicking and froze.

From the swamp, he saw hundreds of glowing orbs that resembled eyes staring back at him, blinking. Between the loud crying, the jet fuel, and the glowing eyes, Nialle had enough and tore out of the spot, leaving just dust from his tires behind.

To this day, people still believe that they hear the cries for help from those 200 lost souls who died there so many years ago.

Chapter 23

Play Ball

The College dorms in our city were pretty old, dating back to when they were originally built in the 1960's. The girl's dorms, especially the lower three floors, hadn't been renovated ever since. The décor was still reminiscent of a time where orange shag ruled the world. The college was the main hub of the sleepy little Ohio town and brought almost all of the city's revenue throughout the year. To attract more students to the ever-expanding University, they decided to take care of the dorms, and get them looking a bit more modern.

As the renovations continued on, they found that some of the college students were either misusing the area for parties when the RA's weren't around, or the area was falling victim to vandalization. The University decided to hire some security from the pool of police officers in the area that were looking for off-duty extra work.

Mitch found the position perfect since he too was finishing up some school, working for the department, and looking for more income.

The shift was more than boring, with the exception of when the bars cleared, but on a normal night, all he did was roam the hallways. There was a lot of interesting old relics from when the dorms were built, and Mitch realized the dorms were initially built to house the girls' softball team, which had won the State Championships every year for ten years. As the programs for the college expanded and the student number increased, they built on to the dorms and allowed normal students to live there.

Mitch had played ball his whole life and was even part of the Police Department's rec league every year. One night, as he was walking the halls, he saw a box filled with old trophies and pictures of the teams. He smiled as he looked through the box, remembering his own days playing collegiate-level baseball. At the bottom of the box was an old Softball, so he picked it up and carried it with him while he roved the floors.

As Mitch entered the second floor, he tripped over a broom that had been left in the floor, and the ball fell from his hands and rolled down the hallway. Before he could grab it, it rolled into one of the empty rooms. He laughed at his own clumsiness and paused as the lights flickered slightly. When he looked back down, the ball was sitting at his feet. He looked around the hallway, walked to the room, and inspected the ball. It was the exact same ball, but there was no one up there with him.

Thinking that someone was messing with him, he laughed and rolled the ball down the hallway. He watched as the ball bounced along the floor but suddenly stopped dead as if someone had stopped it with their hands. He backed up slightly and squinted, watching the ball rise into the air. Still, with his healthy level of skepticism, he didn't really believe what he was seeing.

"Ohhh, big scary ghost," he said laughing, sure that someone was playing a joke on him.

His laughter began to slow as the lights began to frantically flicker around him. Slowly he heard the doors begin to move and they slammed shut, and opened again, creating a really loud banging. He looked back at the floating ball and before he could move, it shot through the air, aimed at his head. He dodged to the right, and the ball hit the wall behind him, leaving quite a dent.

He stepped back slowly as a strong wind whirled through the hallway blowing dust and old papers into the air. The feeling of absolute anger filled his chest, followed by fear of what he was experiencing. Suddenly the winds stopped, and the dust dropped to the floor. From the back, he could hear the tapping of something against the doorframe. With shaking hands, he slowly walked back towards the room. There was no shadow to accompany the obvious movement inside the room, and he slowly turned towards the open doorway. There, hanging from the rafters was the ghostly apparition of a young girl, still wearing her softball uniform and grasping her mitt in her lifeless hand. He began to back up slowly, stepping on a creaky floor beam. The girl, still hanging from the rafters turned her head towards Mitch with an angry look.

Mitch dropped his keys and ran down the stairs and out of the building. Later that night, once calm and safely at home, he did some research on those dorms. Apparently, one of the softball players, just a year before they reassigned the dorms, had been cut from the team, and she proceeded back to the dorms where she hung herself in the hallway. Many students had reported violent hauntings on that wing of the housing including slamming doors, broken mirrors, and screaming in the middle of the night.

Mitch notified the University Dean of what happened, and oddly enough they didn't seem the least bit surprised. A year later, Mitch found out that instead of putting residents on that floor, they turned it into a lounge area for homework and hanging out. There had apparently been "too many instances of paranormal related actions."

Needless to say, he quit the job that night.

Chapter 24

The Locked Door

Lancaster, Pennsylvania is usually known for one thing, the Amish. But little do people realize there is also a bustling Metropolis where an Art School and Christian College are located. All along the still cobblestone streets are row houses and shops, and the sidewalks are packed with wide-eyed art students. The smell of PA's traditional Philly Cheesesteak wafts through the air from a local sub-shop, and the sound of trickling water can be heard from the fountain by the College.

The houses are compact but tall, and most are original designs from decades ago. Lancaster also happens to be one of the ghost capitals of the U.S. with constant stories of apparitional sightings. With the amount of history and real untouched structural heritage, it is no surprise there are so many sightings. The row houses are usually rented for the school year and then left to sit vacant during the summer, except for a couple of older students who stay year-round.

The police force in Lancaster is smaller than the larger metropolis but still large enough to handle the antics of the local college students. Between the artist parties and the rivalry between the two schools, the cops stay pretty busy during the school year. This year, however, one particular house seemed to be either messing with the police, or they were experiencing some really serious supernatural entities. Each time, though, that the girls living in the house would call, by the time they arrived, whatever they thought was going on had stopped.

Officer White had been with the force for thirteen years, and though she usually left those kinds of calls to the newbs, she was interested to find out what was scaring the three girls at 708 Main Street so terribly bad. The girls were all students at the local art school, but they had no history of loud parties or negative behavior. The night the major occurrence happened, it coincided with Halloween night.

As Officer White waded through the crowds of people dressed in the scariest and sluttiest costumes they could find, she pushed to make her way to the girl's row house for the third time that week. The house was located just two blocks from the school and was over a chiropractor office and next to a cigar shop. The only girl home at the time, Alice, met Officer White at the door. She was shaking and clutching on to her cat. She lead Officer White up the long, creaky staircase and into the house. She described the other instances to White such as doors slamming, items in the kitchen falling off shelves, and the sound of someone walking in the front door and up the steps.

Alice explained, in a shaky voice, that most of the occurrences, however, happened while she was in her room. Officer White inspected the apartment but didn't find anything out of the ordinary. She walked back to Alice's room where the girl was visibly shaken and curled up at the back of her bed. The officer felt it necessary to calm Alice before she left, knowing at this point anything was bound to scare her half to death, especially on a full moon Halloween.

As the Officer talked, she couldn't help but notice the sound of faint laughter from the staircase. It seemed Alice didn't notice so she casually peered over the railing, but nothing was there. As she walked back into Alice's bedroom the door slammed behind her, and Officer White pulled her weapon, tugging on the door that seemed to be now locked from the outside. Alice gasped and pulled her knees to her chest yelling, "It's happening again!"

The officer took several steps back and watched as the shadow of someone appeared under the door. The doorknob began to rattle loudly, and out of nowhere, the sound of a train and whistle echoed through the apartment. Sounds of laughter shot from the other side of the room and the walls shook with the force that the door was shaking. Alice covered her ears and screamed.

Then, just as it had started, it all stopped, and a voice rang out.

"Alice?" the voice yelled.

"My roommate," Alice said jumping up and opening the door that now seemed to be fine. She ran out and hugged the girl standing confused at the top of the stairs.

"I heard you scream," she said smiling over at the police officer.

"Did you hear it?" Alice asked frantically.

"No," she said setting her bags down. "Did it happen again? The train?"

Alice shook her head tears streaming down her face. The officer questioned the roommate for a few moments, but she had seen nothing out of the ordinary when she entered the apartment, and no one had come or gone at all. She walked right up the stairs when she heard Alice screaming. Officer White didn't know what to tell the girls, especially since she did her best to hide her hands shaking behind her back.

The girls stayed in the row house until the end of the year, but after what happened, the landlord had a hard time renting to anyone else after that. Officer White pulled up the history of the house back at the precinct and found that original owners had been railroad workers. One day, the man got caught on the tracks and had died. His wife and baby were left without a father and husband, and just two years later, the wife killed herself, leaving the baby to the orphanage.

Officer White stayed researching the case for many years, and later answered a call by new tenants that recalled the same chilling events she had gone through herself. Nothing, however, seemed to chase the ghosts away.

Chapter 25

The Fire of The Lighthouse

On the coast of North Carolina, some of the most beautiful lighthouses can be found. Though some of them have been moved to preserve their heritage, almost all are there for tourists to visit. One lighthouse, however, after a terrifying ordeal with a police officer, has been shut down permanently. The Arcadia lighthouse was once one of the most important ones on the coast. As ships moved through the waterways, they were unable to see Arcadia Island jutting up out of the ground. After several instances of ships running aground on the island in the night, the town decided to install a lighthouse. The lighthouses were run by keepers who would make sure that the flame of the candles that were magnified out to the incoming shifts stayed lit and that the lighthouse stayed safe during hurricane season.

Fast forward several decades later and the Historical Foundation decided to move the lighthouse inland, having no more need due to technological advances in navigation. The lighthouse was set inland and made into a quite popular tourist attraction. They allowed the tourists to climb to the top and see how the lighthouse itself worked, as well as the keeper's living quarters.

However, one sunny day in June the locals observed a woman, dressed in a nightgown walking towards the lighthouse. The tourists glanced at her as she climbed the stairs with them and emerged at the top. No one, however, expected that this woman would set in motion, events that would ultimately shut the lighthouse down. The woman climbed atop the railings, spread her arms wide and jumped from the lighthouse, landing on the cement ground below.

Witnesses to the event say she must have been possessed, as the pupils of her eyes were white as snow and she didn't respond to anyone's calls. Later the police would reveal that the woman was an escaped mental patient from the local inland hospital. Either way, a woman's death marked that hot June day for many onlookers.

Years later, the lighthouse remained a staple in tourist stops along the way to the beaches. Cameras were installed in the top portion due to past vandalism, and a small plaque of remembrance was placed at the top in honor of the woman who had taken her life. Everything seemed pretty quiet at the lighthouse after that.

June Harold was a young officer with the local police and had lived in the Outer Banks her entire life. She had heard of the girl that had taken her life but didn't pay much attention to it. The local Historical Society had asked the police to do some rounds out by the lighthouse throughout the night because they were having an issue with someone breaking in, and the cameras were going dark like they were covering the lens.

June worked the night shift most times and was more than happy to stop through since the tourists in the town weren't very rowdy, and the night shift could be pretty boring. She started the night by swinging through and just doing a regular scan of the premises and checking the doors. The society had given her the keys so she could get inside if need be. They had reported that the occurrences seemed to happen at the same time every day, just before dawn, so June planned to be there at that time, no questions.

The rest of her rounds went fairly well, and she found herself driving up to the lighthouse just before the sun began to lighten the sky from behind the horizon. She parked and got out of her vehicle. As she walked the perimeter, she didn't see anything odd, but as she tugged on the door, which was still locked, she heard the sound of crying inside the lighthouse. June pulled out the keys and swung the door open, but no one was downstairs. She looked around the keyholder quarters for prints but stopped when she heard the creaking of the stairs.

She slowly climbed the lighthouse stairs, calling out to whoever was inside that she was there and they needed to come down immediately. As she walked through the hatch leading to the deck, she paused as a woman in flowing flowery nightgown stood there staring at her. She looked upset, so June put her gun away and talked softly to her.

"Ma'am," she said. "Are you okay? Do you need help?"

The girl just stood there staring at her for a moment before turning and beginning to climb up on the edge of the lighthouse. June slowly walked forward, reaching out for the girl's dress. She froze as the girl turned and grabbed her by the arm, a cold icy chill filled June's chest. The girl's eyes were white as snow, and the expression on her face instantly terrified June. She pulled her arm back and looked down at the blistering skin where the girl's grasp had touched. Before she could react, the girl threw herself over the edge of the lighthouse.

"No!" June screamed out.

She raced over to the edge of the lighthouse and looked down at the cement ground below, but there was no one there. The girl had vanished into thin air. June ran down the stairs and out the door and looked up to where she was just standing, but no one was there. She radioed the station asking that they send the Historical Society out there immediately, she needed to review the tapes.

When the woman arrived, she explained the story to her. The woman's eyes grew big, but she moved to get the tapes for June. They watched them several times, but each time that it was about to show the girl, the tape would go blank. The woman looked down at the blistered skin on June's arm and turned, grabbing a picture from the mantle.

"Was this the girl?" she asked.

June looked down at the old black and white photos, and sure enough, the woman in the picture was the girl she had seen.

"Yes," June exclaimed.

"That's the girl that killed herself several years ago," the lady responded.

June left the lighthouse that day knowing the society was going to close the lighthouse down for good. In fact, just a year later, they bulldozed the building and put a park in its place. Even to this day, though, you can catch a young girl in her nightgown walking gingerly through the park.

Conclusion

As you have seen, true horror stories are all around us. They can happen anywhere, at any time and to anyone. There is no certainty that you will not be living in one of these actual cases yourself. But that is how life is, unknown and full of mysteries, surprising us day by day.

In this book, you encountered a great number of cases. First, an exorcism in Indianapolis, where malevolent evil spirits tormented a helpless family. After support and assistance from several people and a number of exorcisms, the family returned to live a happy and normal life again. You also read about a man that constantly watched over a family, making threats in order for them to leave. Eventually, the family did leave the place and "The Watcher" got what he wanted. Later on, you found out about the strange and puzzling events that took place in a hotel in Los Angeles. A girl there had vanished, and her body mysteriously appeared dead in the water supply tank. This was after she was seen on elevator CCTV footage behaving in a really disturbing manner. Until this day, what happened to Elisa continues to be a mystery to the police. You also read about a family that apparently committed suicide because they believed the world was ending. However, the police found out that they were influenced by a convicted murder and, what they still do not know, is whether their children consented to die with them or not.

Later on, you found out about a voice that called several families in Washington. At first, they thought it was some prank, but they were all wrong, and when they tried to investigate where these calls came from, they appeared to have been made by the same phones owned by the family. To this day, police cannot confirm with certainty the identity of this voice. Then, you read about a couple in London who thought one of their family members was a witch and were determined to make the evil spirits leave their home, no matter what it took. That story ended up very badly, as one of the family members died horribly. Finally, you familiarized yourself with a story of a man that hated God and the church so much that he wanted to take revenge on them by killing two members of the clergy.

As you traveled further into the book, you learned about an officer plagued by the ghosts of past Cancer patients and just how terrifying one red ribbon can really be. You then heard stories of ghosts that seemed to just want to hang out with old ladies, while others were looking for salvation from their killers. Police Officers discovered suicidal apparitions reliving their last moments of torment on this earth and then helping to relieve others by finding their killers. From the case of the crime scene photographer, it does show how much anger can be held where a crime of such hatred and violence has occurred. Even as the living, we can experience the last few moments of life for some of the less fortunate.

These cases, as they are real life events that actually happened, end up in different ways. In some cases, the guilty parties could be found, sentenced and put in jail. However, in other cases, what happened, and the person responsible for the different crimes, remains a total mystery that the police cannot resolve up to this very day.

This is how life is, sometimes with happy endings and sometimes with sad ones, but definitely, it is always more exciting than fiction. Thank you, dear and brave reader, for reaching the end of this book filled with horrible murder and crime cases. I hope you now realize that you should stay awake, alert and always believe what the news says because nowadays, anything is possible, and what sounds too incredible or too horrible to be true, can be waiting for you right around the next corner.

Be safe, dear Reader. But wait, what is that figure behind you now?

Can you help me out?

I'd love to receive your opinion about my book. In the world of book publishing, there are few things more valuable than honest reviews from a wide variety of readers.

Your review will help other readers find out whether my book is for them. It will also be a great help for me in reaching out to more readers and thus, increasing the visibility of my book.

You can leave your review at www.Amazon.com > *digital orders > leave your review* We would appreciate it greatly Thank you

Check out my other books

Chapter 1:

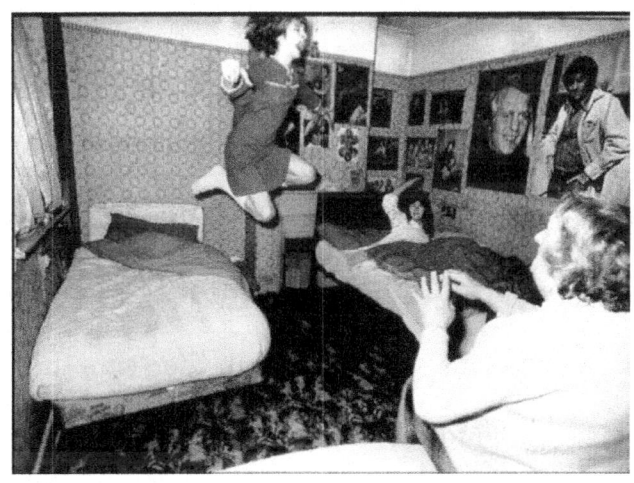

Travails Of The Perron Family

The case of the Perron Family haunting achieved celebrity status thanks to the super success of the Warner Bros movie *The Conjuring* which was largely based on the experiences of this hapless family. The Perrons lived for a decade in a very old house that apparently was home to an unusually large number of spirits of some of its old residents, who though long dead, never left home. It, therefore, fell to the lot of the Perron family to experience the strangest, most bizarre and terribly frightening paranormal phenomena in the years they spent in absolute misery and terror in the company of beings who were not from the world of the living.

The Persons were a large and happy family comprising of Roger Perron, wife Carolyn Perron, and their five young pretty daughters Andrea, Nancy, Christine, Cynthia and April, when they had chanced upon what appeared to them just the right home that the family needed-the picturesque Arnold Estate in Harrisville, Rhode Island. Their troubles with the world of spirits started soon after they bought and moved into, what had appeared to be a lovely country house in the midst of sprawling two hundred acres of land in the year 1970.

Unknown to them at the time of the purchase, the property had a checkered and violent history with many of its old residents, as well as other people from the area, having met with violent ends there. The Perrons, especially the children soon became aware of the presence of a number of spirits, not all of whom were particularly unpleasant, though. There was, however, one particular spirit with a horribly wicked persona who was particularly vicious to Carolyn Perron and made her years in the house excruciatingly painful.

What the children experienced were random nightly disturbances like furniture being dragged across the floor, doors being slammed shut or chillingly even a small child's voice call out for its mother all night long. Though these spirits apparently didn't cause any harm or danger, the impact it must have had on the fragile psyche of small children can be well imagined.

The one who tormented Carolyn was purportedly a practicing witch Bathsheba Sherman who had lived next to the Perron Family home on what was known as the Sherman Farm in the 1800s. Apparently she had had four children, none of whom survived beyond seven years of age, which made the people of the area believe that she had sacrificed her own children to the Devil.

An investigation was ordered into the death of an infant son of hers who it was suspected was done to death by Bathsheba with a sewing needle. No conclusive case however was made out and she was let off. It was the spirit of this person who the Perrons believed had committed suicide by hanging herself from a rafter in their house that had deviously targeted Carolyn with the intent of driving her off the property.

Download the full version book here:

www.NightTerrorPublishing.com/books/

Made in the USA
Las Vegas, NV
03 September 2021